Tom Smith's
CHRISTMAS CRACKERS

Tom Smith's

CHRISTMAS CRACKERS

AN ILLUSTRATED HISTORY

PETER KIMPTON

TEMPUS

To Rose, my bright and shining star, for her love, valued comments and unstinting patience in trying to help me master my computer and for her stoicism in failure!
And for dearest Jess — an outstanding and joyous human being who, although now in her nineties and from an age long since past, is an object lesson to us all with the grace, affection, wit and wisdom she has shown in accepting all that life has sent her way.
God bless you, Jess.
Also for my daughters Rachael and Elizabeth and my grandchildren Isaac and Ezzy, — for the future with my love.

Frontispiece: 'The Cracker Factory.' A brilliant Heath Robinson cartoon showing a fantasy version of cracker production as he imagined it. Page 100 shows the reality in 1984.

First published 2004

Tempus Publishing Limited
The Mill, Brimscombe Port,
Stroud, Gloucestershire, GL5 2QG
www.tempus-publishing.com

© Peter Kimpton, 2004

The right of Peter Kimpton to be identified
as the Author of this work has been asserted in accordance
with the Copyrights, Designs and Patents Act 1988.

British Library Cataloguing in Publication Data.
A catalogue record for this book is available from the British Library.

ISBN 0 7524 3164 1

Typesetting and origination by Tempus Publishing Limited.
Printed in Great Britain.

CONTENTS

The author with partner Rose Tibbles displaying a pair of Victorian style cracker boxes which he designed whilst working for the Tom Smith company in Norwich.

LEGAL DECLARATION

Much of the historical information used in the production of this book is drawn from archive material owned by and the exclusive property of the Kathleen Kimpton Victorian Photographic Archive.

The author is in no way connected to or associated with the present owners of the Tom Smith brand name or trademark, who have had no involvement in the preparation of this book. Any observations in this book are purely the personal thoughts and opinions of the author.

ACKNOWLEDGEMENTS

I gratefully acknowledge the expertise and valued help of a great number of people and organisations – all far more knowledgeable than myself – who have generously given their time and talents in helping me with research and information, and without whose input this book would have been impossible to produce.

In particular, I must mention the following: David Franks, joint managing director of the Mamelok Press, for his most excellent help and advice concerning cracker scraps and other areas; Mr D.R. Richards, general manager of the *Lady* magazine, for his kind permission to use the 1911 'Castle of the Cracker King' article, and Mark Banham of the Islington Local History Centre for unearthing the article originally; advice on cracker snaps was gratefully received from Roy Jackson of Cootes & Jackson For his expertise regarding the use of cracker snaps during the Second World War, I must thank David Penn – Keeper of Exhibits and Firearms at the Imperial War Museum; locally, thanks to Hamish Varnon, the Norwich Records Office, and Sue Pulley of Elite Gift Boxes; in London, thanks to the Victoria & Albert's Archive of Art and Design in the form of Eva White, who went above the normal call of duty to assist; for Selfridge material, I am indebted to former archivist Fred Redding, coupled with the History of Advertising Trust in Norfolk.

Personal recollections were given by Val Bartley, Lily Brown, Matilda Kitson (deceased), Alice Howman and James Grimble (to whom I am grateful for his information regarding the war damage to the Caley factory and the great Tom Smith's fire of 1963): I thank them all.

Similarly, thanks go to Terry Long, until last year one of the directors of the present-day Caley's, and to Joan Rudd (secretary to Eric D. Mackintosh) for information concerning Caley and Caley-Mackintosh. I must particularly mention Mr Bob Morrison, the former chief executive of the Tom Smith company, who generously supplied so much information relating to earlier times. And, for information regarding patents (or lack of them!) sincere thanks to Maria Lampert and the excellent British Library Patents Team for all their searching.

Concerning the work of the great artist A.J. Munnings, I thank Page Bros of Norwich, in the form of managing director David Armstrong and Jan Forkes, for all their help and permission to examine the archives relating to his early cracker box designs for Caley's (while in their employ). Similar thanks must go to Norma Watt of the Norwich Castle Museum for her time and trouble concerning the Munnings work.

Thanks to Christopher Pickup of the Royal Warrant Holders Association and Robert Welton of Rymans; to Derek James of the *Eastern Evening News/Eastern Daily Press* (Archant), again, many thanks for publicising the project, originally together with Simon Tomlinson, Nolan Lincoln and colleagues for their help with archive photographs. I also gladly acknowledge the original research work of Dr Christa Pieske for the 1983 German-language book *Das ABC des Luxuspapiers* and, similarly, Phillip Snyder with his book *December 25*, upon which I have drawn for certain sections of this book. Likewise, I am in the debt of my old school friend Barry Goward, now based in Hamburg, and similarly Christa Braybrooks here in Norwich for assistance with the German translation work. From America, John Grossman, owner of the John Grossman Collection, has generously given his time and knowledge in assisting with historical material relating to crackers in that country, and thanks to Valerie Jackson-Harris of the Ephemera Society here in the UK for putting me in touch with John. I thank them both, together with Amoret Tanner from Reading University.

For the Batger's and other material, I thank the knowledgeable Liz Farrow, poster and ephemera dealer from London, for making it available to me. And finally, for all those people, across the UK especially the good folk of Norwich and Norfolk, who have helped me along the way with various snippets of information and whom, for no good reason other than a failing memory or my own inefficiency, I may have forgotten to mention by name, I offer my sincere thanks.

PREFACE

This is the second history of Tom Smith and the Christmas cracker I have produced – the first, in 1990, was a much more 'potted' version (used for PR purposes), compiled during my time as marketing services manager with the Tom Smith company during the mid-1980s and early 1990s. Much of the material relating to Tom Smith, which you may have seen on various internet sites, has been taken, often verbatim, from that earlier history.

To my knowledge, after some three years research, this is the very first in-depth book on Tom Smith and the Christmas cracker to be published, and in this greatly rewritten, updated and significantly expanded version of my earlier effort, I have included a much wider selection of material and illustrations from both nineteenth and twentieth-century catalogue sources and from my own Kathleen Kimpton archive, which is not generally available to the public. In evaluating material, one of course has to take a view as to whether given information is hard fact or fiction, or whether it has, with the passing of time and by word of mouth, become myth or hearsay. Much of what you see on the internet is exactly that, but I hope the story I have presented is as comprehensive and factual as possible. I have tried very hard to keep within reason the numerous examples of product names and predecimal price points from the many thousands available, even allowing for the fact that company archive material (together with actual physical samples) is relatively thin on the ground.

The contributions from individuals and companies, to whom I am greatly debted, are gratefully acknowledged at the front of this book. With their help, I hope that you enjoy this look back at the world of Tom Smith, the famous invention for which he is traditionally credited and the cracker industry in general. While I have endeavoured to give a flavour of Tom Smith's world of crackers over the years, from his original commercial beginnings in 1840s London up to the present, it is only fair to say that this history can give only the briefest of glimpses into his company's truly vast range of wonderful cracker designs and associated products produced over a period of more than 150 years. It goes without saying that should any reader have or discover any fresh archive material relating to the subject, I would be very pleased to hear from you.

But even though many years have passed since Tom Smith had his original idea, he has certainly not been completely forgotten, especially at Christmas time. In October 1997 the Royal Mail, taking up my original suggestion from the late 1980s, issued a first-day cover comprising five stamps produced by designer John Gorham, based

Ride 'em cowboy! A 1928–29 advert showing Santa as you've never seen him before. This design formed the basis for one of the October 1997 Post Office first-day cover stamps, issued to commemorate the company's 150th anniversary.

Dedication panel from the Smith family memorial fountain in Finsbury Square, London, erected by two of Tom's sons to the memory of their mother – Tom's wife Martha – 1826–1898.

on original Tom Smith's advertising material, to commemorate the company's 150th anniversary. And although they are no longer involved with the company that Tom founded all those years ago – the business now being owned by others – the Smith family is not entirely forgotten. While it is true that there is nothing left of the once great cracker factory in Wilson Street, Finsbury Square in London (see The Castle of the Cracker King – page 124), and with the Norwich premises now being used for other purposes, there is one memorial associated with the family that can still be seen. If you are ever on a trip to London, or if indeed you already live there, put aside just a few minutes to visit the corner of Finsbury Square near Liverpool Street Station, where you will find a drinking fountain which was erected in 1898 by Tom Smith's sons, Tom (junior) and Walter, to the memory of Martha, their mother and Tom's wife. Rather like the history of the company during its last years in Norwich, the fountain is now a little battered and weathered with time, and, although its central figure is missing, this black marble and granite memorial still features typically Victorian dolphins and small grotesque faces. At first sight this twenty-foot-high monolith, in appearance very much like one of the company's own earlier cake decorations, looks as though it came straight out of Highgate Cemetery, and for a drinking fountain it is so highly decorated as to be a fine example of the monumental masons of the day really going to town. With a spire-like top and various pinnacles, this four-sided edifice has drinking troughs on each side – with each being supported by a pair of dolphins. The simple inscription reads:

Erected and presented to the Parish of St Luke by Thomas and Walter Smith (Tom Smith and Co.) to commemorate the life of their mother, Martha Smith. 1826–1898.

A simple enough tribute, but one has to ponder why only the names of two of Tom and Martha's five children appear on this memorial. Nevertheless, what a splendid way to remember one's mother, although such a large, ornate and obviously very expensive memorial must have cost the financial equivalent of hundreds of thousands, if not millions, of crackers. I did wonder if the Smith boys had considered incorporating a cracker or two into the design, but on the grounds of poor taste (and my own suspect sense of humour) I quickly dismissed the idea from my mind! Notwithstanding, it is certainly worth a visit.

* * *

Needless to say, in the world of crackers, some production methods and materials have changed or been updated over time and who can predict what will become of the Christmas cracker over the next 150 years. Indeed, it was only recently that I discovered one Norwich company trading under the name of Elite Gift Boxes, which offers individual presentation crackers made out of tinplate. Managing director Sue Pulley showed me an innovative and attractive range of this variation of the cracker. While not featuring the traditional 'bang', they pull apart exactly as the conventional version but have the added advantage of being supplied empty for the purchaser to fill with contents of their own choice, and can of course be used over and over again. I have a feeling that the creative Mr Smith would have rather liked this novel idea!

Today, many 'modern' crackers, especially from among those being imported from China, are not even tied in the time-honoured manner. These take the form of a very thin sheet of decorated card, which has a series of pre-cut slots and lugs. When rolled into the normal cracker tube shape, the pieces slot together to form a rather stiff, almost synthetic version of the original. Gone are the separately stuck-on scraps, frills and fripperies, to be replaced by pre-printed motifs and design work, all of which combine to replace the traditional hand-made effect we have known for so long. In my opinion, as a traditionalist, 'progress' of this type, as far as the cracker is concerned, is no progress at all.

Nonetheless, personal preferences apart, of all the myriad products, new materials and concepts available in today's market place, few, if any, can match the essential essence of the Victorian period better than the traditional Christmas cracker – albeit with some modern variations. And so when next you visit your local supermarket or department store at the festive season, or indeed at any time, and see all those boxes of colourful crackers piled high, think of the man who, by common consent, invented, designed and gave the cracker its enduring place in our commercial history. We raise our glasses to Tom Smith – the accepted originator of the cracker and the man who put the 'snap' into Christmas.

And as Tiny Tim said, 'God bless us every one' (Charles Dickens, *A Christmas Carol*).

INTRODUCTION

O f all the vast numbers of products that have become part of our everyday lives, the Christmas cracker must stand out as one of the most enduring, especially so at the festive season. This is the story of one man who, from humble beginnings and with vision, drive and determination, built up a massive business based upon confectionery, festive wares and associated material: a man whose name is forever indelibly linked to the Christmas cracker. As one publication in the early 1890s put it somewhat amusingly: 'Tom Smith is the King of Crackers, he stands alone and needs no backers.' An interesting observation, as Tom Smith himself had died by 1881! While the humble cracker could never be described as rocket science, it caught on in a big way. Who indeed would have ever thought that a simple, easily constructed coloured paper tube containing a little motto, verse or gift and fitted with a small banging device and various little items of decoration would have become such a tradition? Indeed, I don't think it would be altogether wide of the mark to call the cracker the ultimate throwaway product!

It is for the conception, birth and development of the Christmas cracker that Tom Smith, confectioner and entrepreneur, does indeed stand alone. Having gone public with his basic bonbon-based idea in the late 1840s, albeit with the initial non-exploding version, little in his wildest dreams would he have imagined how his product would catch the public imagination and that, over 150 years on, it would still be going strong. In social terms, not only has the Christmas cracker given work and support to countless families and contributed in no small way to the economy over the years, it has, just as importantly, provided basic, simple pleasure to many millions which, at the end of the day, is surely what the cracker is all about.

Some historical notes suggest that another Londoner, a Mr Hovell from Holborn, was the real inventor of the Christmas cracker and was manufacturing in 1854. Other reference material from the early 1850s also mentions an Italian who was supposed to have been credited with the invention, but I will refer to these two gentlemen later. Nevertheless, whatever the truth of the matter, it is Tom Smith who, either in fact or by his own self-promotion, gained the kudos for the invention. However, it is ironic that it was Hovell's of Maidstone who eventually took over the Tom Smith company in Norwich in 1985.

It is also an interesting coincidence that during the early Victorian period and while Tom Smith was developing his idea, Prince Albert had arrived in England to marry Queen Victoria, and it was he who introduced the German tradition of the Christmas tree. In its turn, this tradition, along with the cracker, has also become part of the Christmas celebration in many countries throughout the world.

A charming Victorian family Christmas scene featuring, of course, the ubiquitous box of Tom Smith's crackers in the foreground as viewed in the London Illustrated News *of 1893. By kind permission of Malcolm Warrington.*

The Christmas cracker has today, at the beginning of the twenty-first century, spread its wings across the globe to a multitude of very different societies that hold a wide range of religious beliefs. Happily it transcends any religious considerations to provide simple and wholesome fun, pleasure and tradition not only at the festive season but at many different types of function throughout the year.

In English terms, Christmas crackers are as traditional and well known as fish and chips, roast beef and Yorkshire pudding, the Boat Race, morris dancing and all those things that combine to colour and enhance our distinctive character and traditions as a nation. Christmas celebrations, as we know them today, would just not be the same without the good old cracker.

A NOTE ON THE ARCHIVE MATERIAL

From its inception until 1941, Tom Smith's had accumulated a substantial archive of cracker boxes, cracker samples and much associated material in their London factory, but sadly about a third of the factory and almost the entire archive was completely destroyed in the Blitz of that year. All this was on top of an earlier fairly extensive fire that took place in the 1930s, as confirmed by Bob Morrison, the company's one-time chief executive. A similar fate befell the old rival Caley (by this time Mackintosh's) factory in Norwich between 27 and 29 April 1942 when Hitler's boys once again did their worst and much of the factory was destroyed* (although the cracker-making block escaped major destruction).

While one has to admit that although historical material regarding the cracker industry is relatively sparse compared with what once existed, there is still enough of it to make any serious research well worthwhile.

Today, the Tom Smith's original archive would have been an utterly priceless resource but, among the sadly small amount of material that is left, there are still some really wonderful items. These may be found in the main in the Victoria & Albert Museum in London, the Felissimo Christmas Archive in Japan, the Robert Opie Collection, the History

---

* In the main, while some of the factory was indeed destroyed by direct bombing as a result of the German Baedeker raids, certainly parts of the complex, so I have been told by ex-employees, were destroyed by the fires that had spread from nearby burning buildings.

A general view of 1942 Second World War damage to the Caley's factory at Chapel Field in Norwich.

Total devastation – more war damage at Chapel Field. In footballing terms it was Luftwaffe 1, Caley's 0!

of Advertising Trust in Norfolk (for Selfridge material), the Rickard Centre of Ephemera Studies at Reading University and within my own archive here in Norwich. For reference to 'scraps', the archives of the Mamelok Press of Bury St Edmunds in Suffolk house some amazing and beautiful material (see page 42 and colour section).

Among the material now housed in the V&A is a selection of beautiful, very fragile and yet basically intact cracker boxes in an assortment of sizes, a number of which I featured in the company's 1991 catalogue, and an assortment of trade brochures that were placed there by the company on permanent loan to the museum in the late 1990s. A full listing of the V&A's cracker archive, which contains varying amounts of assorted material relating to a number of the companies mentioned in this book, can be found in the museum's Archive of Art and Design. A further selection of some fifty-plus cracker boxes and associated material is also to be found within the Robert Opie Collection.

It is also no coincidence that in quite a few instances, I mention the firm of A.J. Caley of Norwich, with whom Tom Smith's merged in 1953. Because of that link, a fair amount of local Caley's material and information was uncovered in the preparation of this book, much of which I have included.

Batger's is another name which is worth inclusion, with this particular manufacturer being one of the few of Tom Smith's competitors whose creative box graphics came anywhere near to matching their own. With thanks to Liz Farrow in London, my own collection now features a superb selection of Batger's unused second-cost material in the form of box labels, mainly from the 1925 to 1930 period, which, she tells me, were originally stored in a barn somewhere! A goodly number of Batger's labels show an almost naïve quality to the drawing and graphics but, many offer examples of really skilful and lively artistic work. It is also worth mentioning that Batger's appear to have joined those companies who were not averse to a spot of plagiarism, in that a number of their designs bore more than a passing similarity to some of Tom Smith's own work.

Another source which has yielded some interesting research material is the German-language book *Das ABC des Luxuspapiers* published in Berlin in 1983 by Deitrich Reimer Verlag, with the main author being Dr Christa Pieske (whose research I gladly acknowledge and to which I refer in various places). The book was produced as a catalogue for an exhibition on paper products for the period 1860–1930 held between July 1983 and February 1984 at the Museen für Deutche Volkskunde, Staatliche Museen Preussischer Kultubesitz, in Berlin.

The archives also give some indication that Tom Smith's seems to have been something of a tolerant company, at least on occasion. There is an interesting account in the Victoria & Albert Museum records, which covers the dishonesty of one of the company's employees as reported in the 'Confectioners Union' of 1909 and which is summarised as follows:

A travelling salesman for the firm of Tom Smith's [allegedly a Mr J.H. Penott] who was taken on in 1899, had a fondness for drink. In 1903, he was suspended for a misappropriation of £35 but was reinstated after writing letters of repentance and repeated promises to lead a different life (he had a wife and five children). He was suspended again in 1906 for further misappropriation of another £40 but was again reinstated and was offered £20 if he promised to abstain from drink completely. He declined this offer and even persuaded the firm to allow him to keep a bottle of whiskey for medicinal purposes. By 1908, his ill-gotten gains were found to have risen to £100 [a pretty considerable sum in those days]. He was watched for a week before his arrest and he was seen always to call at a public house before calling upon a customer. He was sentenced to six months in prison of which he only served five and, during which time Tom Smith's surprisingly paid an allowance to his wife and children. Even after what seems to have been this more than fair attitude on the part of the company, he continued to cause trouble for the firm by spreading false rumours about the way the company had treated him!

Maybe the charitable actions of the company towards the man's family give a tiny clue to the ethical nature of the Tom Smith family (when this event took place) or maybe, despite his drink problem, the man was such a good representative that the company didn't want to lose his services. We can only speculate the reason.

Much of the historical information used in the production of this book is also drawn from exclusive archive material from the Kathleen Kimpton Victorian Photographic Archive.

While many people have heard of the man and know his products, almost nobody has any idea as to what he looked like – until now that is. It was while examining the company archives when they were still housed at its premises in Norwich that I discovered possibly the only known commercial picture of the great man himself – a surprisingly formal and unsmiling pose for someone who had become known as a purveyor of 'fun' products. Certainly today's marketing and promotional people would have used such a photo opportunity in a much more flamboyant way, but lest we forget, Victorian times were indeed somewhat different and considerably more formal than our own.

CHAPTER ONE

WHERE DID IT ALL BEGIN?

Within this history of the Christmas cracker, we shall explore the Tom Smith story, his commercial beginnings, how his business developed, the type of product he produced and sold in his heyday, his competitors and his awareness of the current trends, which in turn affected what he produced and when he produced it within his extensive range of designs and products. We will also look at beautiful graphic examples of his company's advertising material.

While nothing at this point in time gives us any clue as to the Tom Smith company's earlier sales and distribution strategy, it is interesting to look back at its simple, indeed some might say unsophisticated, approach, which although making use of traditional price points as today, seems to have relied very much on the fine box graphics to give the company an edge!

The great majority of people today will have absolutely no idea of how vast was the range of products that Tom Smith stocked: it included Christmas crackers, confectionery, bunting, banners, flags of nations, masks, giant crackers, party products, table and cake decorations for weddings, together with tinplate and china novelties. The crackers were originally called Cosaques – a name which seems to have lasted for about ten to fifteen years – and it is interesting, and rather puzzling, that during the late 1870s Tom Smith's were featuring both crackers and Cosaques in their product catalogues at the same time.

I have yet to discover why they ran these two names in tandem, but my guess is that at that time their crackers had indeed come to be called 'Crackers', and the name 'Cosaque' was then applied to their ornate table decoration crackers. This seems to be borne out in part by the fact that Caley's, a major competitor, was, even as late as 1923, offering a range of over fifty 'Art Cosaques' – table decorations that were a stunning selection of fancy and frilly wonders, with the Festive, Poppyland, Butterfly and King Bruce designs standing out from the crowd. It seems strange that Caley's should continue to use an outdated name for so long; Tom Smith's had certainly dropped the name by the time their 1891–92 catalogue was issued.

The basic crackers in those earlier times were initially rather smaller than those of today, often quite plain and about six inches long with many having fringed ends. They got the name of Cosaques, so it has been said, on the basis that many Victorians who used them had the strange idea that when being pulled, the novelties sounded similar to the crack of whips used by the Cossacks as they rode through Paris during the Franco-Prussian War. However, one must ask: (1) who would have stopped and drawn the similarity while being in the middle of a war zone with, possibly at times, shells whistling overhead and (2) how many everyday Victorians would have actually been travelling in France during that particular war? But whatever the source, Cosaques they became for some years.

Even a very brief look through the Tom Smith's archive material will immediately convey just how astute, commercially aware, flexible and extremely up to date the company was in its choice of design subject and graphics. One can only look in awe at what was, for many years, an astonishing and comprehensive range of wonderful designs, covering such topical subjects as films, transport, sport, politics, science, royalty, fashion and the military to name but a few. Of course, for countless years, using these fine labels meant that the customer couldn't actually see the product inside the box – a practice which has totally changed in today's marketplace with most current packaging giving the customer full view of what they are getting!

The only known commercial picture of Tom Smith himself – from the 1850s / 1860s.

WHO WAS TOM SMITH?

Information about the man himself has proved elusive to say the least and I am forced to speculate to some degree. We certainly know about his invention and products, we can view surviving examples of his packaging and advertising, and we have an actual picture of him yet Tom Smith and his origins remain something of a mystery. Little, if anything, is known today about his family background apart from him being a Londoner who, as far as I can tell, must have started his working life between 1834 and 1836 at around the age of twelve to fourteen – not at all young for those times. Some sources refer to him being an actual pastry cook or a baker but, whilst he could have been, nothing has come to light to prove or disprove this one way or another.

While we know that Tom's wife Martha (mistakenly referred to by some as Mary) was born in 1826 and died in 1898, searches in the traditional registers of births, marriages and deaths if nothing else unearth the not unsurprising fact that there were many with the surname of Smith and many of them sported the Christian names of either Thomas (Tom) or Martha. The notion of searching for needles in haystacks thus rapidly comes to mind!

It seems reasonably likely, however, that Tom and Martha were married around 1845 to 1846 when she was probably in her late teens or early twenties, and that they both worked together in the newly formed business, which was formally established in 1847. Assuming that Tom was just a little older than Martha, it would mean that he was probably born in the early 1820s.

Reference to the 1881 census registered at Hampstead, however, reveals that Tom was no longer in the land of the living by that date, with his wife Martha being listed as the head of the household. Also included by name in this census are his five children: Thomas, 32 (b. 1849); Henry, 30 (b. 1851); Walter, 27 (b. 1854); Martha, 23 (b. 1858) and Lilly, 22 (b. 1859), with their address being given as 105 King Henry Street.

The fact that Tom is not mentioned in this particular census tells us that he must have died in his fifties or very early sixties, which is not a total surprise as he must have put so much of himself into his ever-expanding business. With all the stresses and strains that pushing the business forward must have involved, it appears that he literally worked himself into a relatively early grave.

But to revert back to his beginnings: as previously mentioned, Tom had been apprenticed to a now unknown London baker and confectioner probably somewhere between 1834 and 1836. In this time he would have learned to make such things as fancy goods, and in particular cake decorations, which involved pouring liquid icing sugar into boxwood moulds to be knocked out when set. Just a few of these types of moulds survive today, and those which I personally have seen, as with many artefacts from the past, attest to the skills of whoever carved them.

Like many apprentices, Tom's working life of initial learning and practice became a life of expertise. His own developing skills and advancement within the company certainly meant that he arrived at a point in his life when he decided, like many young men, that he could do better on his own. And, of course, being one's own boss always has a certain appeal! In his spare time, he had been successfully experiment-ing with and improving certain items (probably mainly in the area of cake decorations and ornaments) to the extent that he felt confident enough to try his luck and set up in business on his own account from premises at Goswell Road in Clerkenwell, East London.★ After a

★There is also reference of the company having had premises at 8 Fredericks Place in 1847 when it advertised 'Confections' and after 1847 when it advertised 'Wholesale Confectionery' from the same address. Whether this address was used at the same time as the Goswell Road site or whether, after the latter had become too small, it was the sole operating premises prior to the move to Wilson Street is unknown. Possibly it was even a showroom or warehouse but what is certain, however, is that Wilson Street was in use by the company in 1873. The 1875 company catalogue also alludes to 'late of 320 & 322 City Road EC,' so this also seems to have been another premises from which Tom Smith operated.

relatively short period of time, as we now know, the business went from strength to strength. While extensive searches have failed to yield the actual date when he moved to Goswell Road, these premises appear to have been an ordinary residential terraced house and it could well be that Tom and his wife were living over the shop.

FOREIGN TRAVELS

Certainly Tom, like many enterprising businessmen today, would have quite often visited trade fairs and retail outlets, looking for new ideas both at home and abroad. It is likely that on one such trip to Paris (possibly while on holiday) that he came across the extremely profitable bonbon. Goodies – probably sugared almonds – had been wrapped in wax or tissue paper, twisted at the ends by Parisian confectioners or *bonbonniers*. The presentation immediately caught Tom the confectioner's eye to the extent that having spotted a potential opportunity he decided to copy it and incorporate the idea into his own product range back home in England.

BONBONS BACK HOME

On his return home to London and just a few weeks before Christmas that year, he obtained the basic materials of tissue paper and sugared almonds, and had his staff produce what was to become probably the first supply of bonbons to be offered for sale in England.

His hunch proved right but while these bonbons achieved very acceptable sales during that Christmas period, they dropped away after the festive season and he was left to fall back on his basic product range of wedding cake decorations and fancy ornaments, together with confectionery. To stimulate trade, he came up with the idea of placing a small motto or rhyme within the bonbon. This addition was possibly based on the original Chinese August Moon Festival concept of giving moon cakes (made from lotus nut paste) which contained messages expressing good wishes or portents of good fortune.*

*This custom had originally come into being during the thirteenth and fourteenth centuries when China was occupied by the Mongols. The Chinese smuggled messages to each other inside the cakes (the Mongols supposedly not liking the taste!) and continued until the time of the building of the railways across America during the 1840s to 1860s by many Chinese immigrant workers who had carried this traditional custom with them. Today, the tradition continues around the world in the form of what we know today as the Fortune Cookie.

This timescale for the bonbons links approximately with the period from the mid 1840s and into the following decade when Tom Smith was developing his cracker idea and there seems to be a very fair chance that this is when he got the idea of including his little messages or rhymes within his crackers. Not an absolutely hard fact but it has some credence. In a light-hearted moment, one can also perhaps imagine Tom going down to his local tavern and his friends saying, 'Hello Tom, still messing around with those silly paper things? They'll never catch on you know, you're wasting your time!' Well, how wrong can you be?

By implementing his idea of double wrapping, he was successfully able to insert a motto – usually a love motto, to the amusement and delight of many of his young lady customers no doubt. You can imagine perhaps the stifled giggles and maybe the blush of some airy young lady who had picked the motto or love verse that predicted that her future would lie with a handsome young man! Chapter Four illustrates what these flowery little declarations of love typically used to say. The inclusion of mottos was followed by small trinkets or baubles, again with immediate success. Typical examples of these verses can be seen in Chapter Four and are reproduced from early trade catalogue entries which, for the benefit of potential buyers, offered sample verses with the rhymes invariably reflecting the subject of the design on the cracker box lid.

CHAPTER TWO

SNAPS 'N' SCRAPS

Although the basic concept of the cracker was in place at this point, further work was needed. Over the next few years, during the 1850s, Tom experimented in various ways to improve his range, but the one idea that really made him his fortune was his invention of the cracker 'snap', as it is known within the cracker industry. The traditional story tells that once, while sitting in front of an open fire, Tom threw on another log (or disturbed an already burning one), which began to pop and spit as the gasses were released. This mini 'explosion' gave him the idea of introducing a bang into the make-up of his bonbons. It seems to have taken Tom around two years to evolve a good working 'snap', and very possibly some degree of personal injury while striking the right balance of explosive material. Too little may not have been such a problem, but too much and who knows?

A good working snap, as may be seen today, is achieved by pulling apart two toughened strips of paper or thin board that have been coated on one end with coarse but mildly explosive chemical material. The two coated ends are bound together at the centre with a small Manila paper wrap to form one long strip, with the explosive portion in the middle. When the strip is pulled from either end, friction is caused as the strips are ripped apart and the explosive material is ignited, thus causing a small bang or 'snap'.

Whether the story of the spitting log is really true, again we shall never know for sure but it is the one which nearly everybody seems to accept and so, for the sake of this history, I shall follow the majority as it would seem a little churlish to dismiss such a cosy little piece of folklore.

Experimentation over, in around 1860, our intrepid inventor was able to offer to the public his 'Bangs of Expectation'.

It is important to consider the subject of patents, relating to Tom Smith in particular. Many sources refer to Tom Smith as having taken out a patent on his idea in the mid to late 1840s. The fact of the matter is, however, that he was unable to patent the basic cracker as he himself had taken the idea from the bonbons that he had seen in France. The concept therefore would have been deemed to have already been in the public domain and therefore not patentable. This information was supplied to me by the excellent and resourceful British Library Patents Team. After an exhaustive search of their records, they were able to confirm that had he wanted, he would have been perfectly at liberty to have patented his snap idea but, for whatever reason, he appears not to have done so. Surprisingly, it seems, neither did anybody else!

It has been suggested that Tom Smith originally produced all his own snaps (and maybe he did) but such was the extent of his growing cracker range and the quantities involved that the company subsequently sourced its snaps from independent outside suppliers. While sadly the names of these very early suppliers have been lost in time, it is nonetheless certain that from the early part of the 1920s the company's requirements were met by both the Acme Board & Paper Co. and similarly by the Reliance Snap Co. of Bishop's Stortford, both of whom were main suppliers to the ever-expanding cracker industry at that time, with Caley's and Hovell's also being but two of their major customers. Sadly, Reliance ceased to trade in around 1987 and currently there is only one company that supplies snaps to the UK cracker trade: Cootes & Jackson of Wetherby, who import solely from China.

In the early days, it appears that saltpetre (potassium nitrate) was the chemical used to achieve the mini explosion. In today's scenario, the 'bang' associated with the snap is produced under friction by the chemical called silver formalate which, under current safety restrictions (BS 7114), can be no more than 1.6 milligrams per unit.

As with all things, the safety regulations in Victorian times were certainly not what they are today and during my time with Tom Smith's, I did hear that in the early days, news reports singled out shadowy smaller, usually unnamed organisations or individuals who had produced crackers in which the snap actually caught fire when pulled. If these rumours were in any way based upon fact then for some folk, Christmas at that time must have indeed gone with a bang, and maybe the turkey was a little overdone that year!

CRACKER SCRAPS

The subject of cracker scraps in particular, and Victorian scraps in general, is a very large one and very much a case for a completely separate study in its own right. An excellent book on the subject is *The History of Printed Scraps* by Alistair Allen and Joan Hoverstadt (New Cavendish Books), which offers an illuminating insight into the subject which is so evoca tive of the Victorian age.

As is well known, the Victorians were very keen on collecting scraps and there were many companies producing and selling albums to accommodate this craze. Today they often turn up at antique fairs, sales and specialist auctions and it is not unusual to see scraps stuck all over Victorian dressing screens and other items of furniture of the period in which capacity they become part of the activity better known as découpage.

For much of the history of the product, crackers have featured small paper decorations which were either attached to the main body of the cracker or, in the more distant past, attached to the 'handles' also. These small decorative pictures, millions of which finished up in the aforementioned scrapbooks, also became known as 'scraps' in cracker trade parlance, with the name continuing within the industry to the present day. These scraps, along with much of the discarded commercial material and product wrappings of the time, which we today so like to refer to as 'ephemera', were most certainly welcome additions to the scrapbooks of both the rich and poor alike in those times. Fine examples of cracker scraps are to be seen in Smith's 'Birds, Beasts and Fishes' box, Tom Smith's No. 930 – Egyptian-style crackers (with the lid design featuring for some reason a most wonderful large green crocodile swallowing a cracker almost as big as itself and closely attended by a cross-legged Egyptian and with pyramids in the background!) and the superb pale blue 'Wedgwood Art Crackers', which feature traditional Wedgwood classical statuettes (or Muses) in a variety of poses. Where these particular original scraps were actually sourced is today unknown but in later years, it is not beyond the realms of possibility that at least a proportion of the company's requirements were designed and produced by Smith's own Smith Val Rosa company in London. Even up to 1930, the company was listed as chromolithographic printers, artists and designers, as well as publishers and stationers. In more recent times still, the company used many scraps that were printed by and purchased from the Mamelok Press of Bury St Edmunds, England – fine specialist printers in this field.

Even at the time when Tom Smith was inventing his cracker, scraps were well established and throughout the nineteenth century as a whole it was astonishing just how many printers, publishers and designers of these items there were in the world (although mainly in Europe). Allen & Hoverstadt's book lists the figure as being in excess of 300!

Many of the very best scraps were produced both in the UK and especially Germany (where they are known as *Oblaten*) and the sheer numbers, which must have run into hundreds or even thousands of millions, together with associated products, such as the albums, were universally available. The appetite for these vast quantities during the Victorian era was only matched by the ubiquitous photographic *cartes de visite* which, in the late 1850s to their zenith in the 1860s, were selling in the region of 300 to 400 million per year. On numerous occasions I have found the odd scrap tucked inside a number of *cartes de visite* albums of the period being offered for sale.

The quality of scraps coming out of Germany in particular during the nineteenth century was superb, and the self-same printing skills which had contributed to that excellence were put to further use in the production of fine postcards, which themselves were to become yet another great Victorian collecting craze during the last quarter of the nineteenth century and extending certainly up until the First World War. These postcards in their turn were again produced by the million, with many marked 'Printed in Saxony'. Bearing in mind Tom Smith's ability to respond to current events, I think the company must have missed a trick here as I have never come across reference to any crackers which they produced tying in with the postcard craze, and this for a company which was always so quick to associate itself with popular trends! Having said that, many of Smiths Edwardian period crackers featured scraps depicting images of pretty young ladies – very similar to those appearing on the postcards of the day.

It seems almost unfair to single out one scrap manufacturer over another as standards were so good, but names which rank among the better known include P.B. Zoecke, E.A. Schwerdtfeger, Raphael Tuck, S. Hildesheimer & Co., Albrecht & Meister and of course Mamelok who, while originating in Breslau, Germany, in 1927, moved to the UK in 1936. Sadly, from those many printers of the nineteenth century, Mamelok is the only remaining supplier of scraps in the UK today and one of just a very small handful of specialist companies across the whole world who still produce these traditional items. Even a very brief look through the current Mamelok catalogue shows them still to be producing fine reproductions of a large number of the earlier Victorian and Victorian style scraps and associated material – well worth a look!

So where does this leave Tom Smith in terms of when he first started to use scraps? Unfortunately, specific information has been impossible to find. However, my own educated guess is that he got the idea from Germany: many bakers and confectioners in that country, certainly around the 1830s to 1850s, used to decorate biscuits, cakes and other goodies with small reliefs for special occasions such as Christmas, Easter, weddings, births, christenings, confirmations and deaths. As we have previously discussed, our intrepid cracker maker often travelled around, seeking new ideas and viewing what the rest of the world was up to, and with his own background in bakery and confectionery, it has to be at least a reasonable assumption that he must have become aware of what his German counterparts were doing, which could conceivably have given him the idea to add scraps to his crackers.

PRINTING & EPHEMERA

Today, probably most if not all cracker manufacturers buy in their advertising and packaging material requirements from outside suppliers – as did the Tom Smith company in later years. However, the middle years of the company were different. Not only did Tom Smith's produce its own cracker boxes in London (as was the case at the time of the merger with Caley's of Norwich), but the company also had its own printing firm, Smith Val Rosa & Co., which was responsible for the production of a good deal of the company's printing needs. This was initially by the chromolithographic method and they produced countless numbers of truly wonderful box designs, annual company

A selection of Caley cracker scrap designs taken from a 1935 company in-house magazine. Not tip-top quality in aesthetic terms but typical of the period.

sales brochures, price lists and possibly at least some of the company's scrap requirements. The earlier years of the 1870s had also seen the printing firm of T. Williams of Kings Cross, London, supplying at least some of Smith's catalogue requirements.

While today there are still fairly numerous examples of scraps and scrapbooks around, sadly relatively few examples of the wonderfully printed period cracker boxes and box labels have survived and those that have can often command premium prices in auctions and at antique fairs. In 1992 I saw a box of just six fancy Caley's Table Decoration crackers, in very nice condition, on offer for the amazingly high sum of £150 at an antiques fair in Peterborough. Due to their fragility, truly antique boxes of early crackers are, if not impossible, very difficult to find either damaged or undamaged, and they rarely come to light. However, as with all areas of collecting, you can always be lucky and unearth the odd bargain! Also, at that same Peterborough fair, I was just about to leave, when I spotted a few stalls that I had not yet visited. For some reason, I decided to have a quick look and there, tucked away under a table, almost hidden from view, I had the almost unimaginable piece of luck. In an old box, I found a quantity of the company's wonderful old trade catalogues and even a couple of their old share certificates, all of which had somehow survived in very good condition and which have yielded so much valuable information in the compilation of this history. What the catalogues were doing in Peterborough we will never know but maybe, just maybe old Mr Smith had a hand in it!

CHAPTER THREE

VARIETY
& MORE VARIETY

Whatever else may be said about Tom Smith's, one has to acknowledge the sheer variety of their designs – a variety which today, due to the fiercely competitive nature of the industry and marketing methods, sadly is no longer possible.

It is impossible to tell whether in his heyday Tom used artists employed directly by the company or bought in his designs from outside sources or a combination of both. Whatever the source, the quality of the huge number of box illustrations used on his products was absolutely superb and they pay a wonderful visual tribute to those, now long gone, who created them.

It would be fair to say that many of the company's box designs reflected something akin to a glow of the Victorian British Empire and often showed direct colonial influence. Designs such as Empire Crackers, Japan–British Exhibition, the Royalty Box of Crackers, Indian Empire Crackers, the Rajah's Jewel Box and Young India Crackers all added an imperialistic touch.

On the subject of crackers with a colonial flavour, I must briefly refer once again to the firm of Batger & Co., which produced crackers for many years. Sometime between 1895 and 1903, Batger's produced a most wonderful box label design for their 'Colonial' Crackers (No. 468) featuring, in a central oval, a rather stern-looking portrait of the government minister Joseph Chamberlain (a very powerful supporter of colonialism and father of Neville). He, in turn, is surrounded with various multi-coloured flags and shields featuring coats of arms of such worthy places as Canada, New Zealand and New South Wales. Under the portrait of Chamberlain is the very typically Victorian statement of 'One Flag – One Empire'. This design is really rather a clever piece of marketing by Batger's in that they were linking their product with one of the best-known politicians of the day to gain extra kudos and thus hopefully increased sales both in the heart of and the wider reaches of the British Empire. The results of their efforts are unknown.

In terms of self-promotion, one can imagine what a wonderful piece of PR it would have been for Tom Smith had there been any photographs showing the Royal family using his products in those earlier days and I'm sure he would have made good promotional use of them, but sadly, even after some thirty years as a student and collector of Victorian photographic images, my research has failed to turn up any pictures of that nature. Even the Royal photographic archive at Windsor drew a blank on this one. The fact that Prince Albert left this life in 1861 would surely have meant that Victoria, entering her prolonged period of mourning, would have had little inclination to celebrate anything, let alone use the increasingly popular Christmas cracker. Although there are no known early photographs of people using crackers, Amoret Tanner of Reading University advises that five greetings cards in their archive from around 1870 to 1880 show designs featuring crackers.

A SELECTION OF
Tom Smith's
Themed Box Designs

FEATURING

Sports, Racial/Ethnic, Royalty, Empire, Patriotic, Topical & Wartime Subjects

1906–1931

Strange goings-on at the golf course. In the comic 'Golfing Crackers' the young caddy gets a whack on the head and the tee has become a cracker. The golfer in his plus fours and spats cuts an amusing figure in this 1906-07 design. Price: 21s per dozen boxes.

Five for the price of one. The company produced many sporting designs over the years but here in 'All Sports' the customers got rugby, tennis, swimming, hockey and cricket for their money! Price: 48s per dozen boxes.

LEFT *The sailor and the grinning black man appear to be doing a spot of bartering in 'Darkie's Surprise' as the grass-skirted figure and our seafaring friend exchange crackers for beads in this 1930–31 box. Price: 40s per dozen boxes.*

RIGHT *Traditional 'jazz' is on offer here with a New Orleans-style, dinner-suited and tailed negro band in real swinging style from 1925–26. The contents in these crackers were based on musical instruments with strangely named 'Humaphones' and 'Syrens' being listed. Price: 34s per dozen boxes.*

LEFT *'Sambo Crackers' from 1930–31 shows a smiling black saxophone player. The shirt on this gentleman of rhythm gives the distinct impression of him being a convict! Price: 34s per dozen boxes.*

RIGHT *Not a jam jar in sight on this occasion. This 1910–11 design at the cheaper end of the range, depicts a traditional golliwog (invariably associated with the Robertson company) holding an even smaller puppet. Price: 6s 9d per dozen boxes.*

In 1910–11, loyalty to the crown was undoubtedly somewhat stronger than it is today and in this 'Royalty' box we see a much-decorated George V. The scraps in this box feature other prominent members of the Royal family of the day. Price: 42s per dozen boxes.

The very popular Edward Prince of Wales (Edward VIII) featured in 'Our Charming Prince' where he is shown in a smiling, uniformed stance together with flying and golfing poses in this 1930–31 presentation. No sign of Mrs Simpson on this one! Price: 42s per dozen boxes.

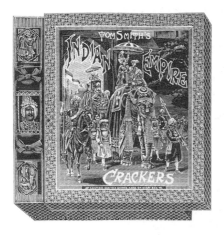 

LEFT *Decorated elephants carrying dignitaries and accompanied by troops are portrayed in this 1910–11 'Indian Empire' box. Price: 42s per dozen boxes.*

RIGHT *The 'Young India' design of 1928–29 displays a marching line of turbaned young Indian men shouldering crackers instead of rifles! Price: 52s per dozen boxes.*

LEFT *Just a simple yet effective portrayal of the Union flag in this 1917 box of 'Patriotic Crackers' emphasises the message of patriotism in the Empire. Price: 16s per dozen boxes.*

RIGHT *'Colonial Crackers' from 1917 show colonial military scenes featuring Canadian, South African and Australian guardians of the Empire. Price: 16s per dozen boxes.*

LEFT *Crowds of folk in evening dress stare in amazement at the cracker radio mast in this 1906–07 'Marconi Messages' design with radio waves radiating in all directions. Price: 21s per dozen boxes.*

RIGHT *The 1910–11 box entitled 'Suffragette Crackerettes' pictures a stern lady with rolled umbrella exhorting her audience to 'Vote for Tom Smith.' Who would dare not to!? Price: 16s per dozen boxes.*

LEFT *Curious crowds gather to watch three ladies in the political 'Votes for Women' design. With Westminster in the background, note the placard wording – 'Votes for women and no police' – offered in 1917. Price: 18s per dozen boxes.*

RIGHT *The 'Channel Tunnel' so long a dream on both sides of 'la Manche' is reflected here in this 1930–31 box with an English John Bull and a French Marianne pulling a cracker together. The oncoming train emerging from the yet-to-be constructed tunnel seems far too close for comfort! Price: 16s per dozen boxes.*

LEFT *'Trophies of the War' (1917) shows an English Tommy to be a bit of a looter. We see him here laden down with the spoils of war and a rather crestfallen German Imperial eagle on a lead in tow behind. Price: 40s per dozen boxes.*

RIGHT *Again in 1917 Tom Smith's 'Big Gun Crackers' were on offer depicting a battery of English troops shelling the enemy. Price: 18s per dozen boxes.*

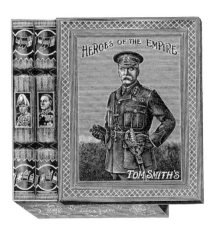

LEFT *Also a 1917 presentation was 'Heroes of the Empire.' The box lid features what appears to be Lord Kitchener with the scraps on the individual crackers inside the box also featuring other military 'worthies' such as Admiral Jellicoe, Sir John French, Rear Admiral C.E. Madden and so on. Price: 36s per dozen boxes.*

RIGHT *The Royal Navy was not forgotten either with 'British Navy Crackers'. A 1917 design, it depicts a powerful British destroyer being overflown by some form of seaplane. Price: 36s per dozen boxes.*

All the fun of the ball or 'masques' as the Victorians used to call them. Here we have a selection of hat and face masks based upon those from the period. Material by kind permission of the Mamelok Press.

The Victorians were very fond of parties and, during the Christmas period, many were held – often being known as masques at that time. A reference from 1884 shows a 'Noah's Ark' selection with masks of animal heads and similarly 'Character' crackers accompanied by masks depicting such worthies as the Prince of Wales, Mr Gladstone, Lord R. Churchill, Mr Henry Irving, Sarah Bernhardt and Mr Bradlaugh. It was at these functions that guests would use these types of masks, fancy dress and of course crackers, but many parties and especially those held on Twelfth Night were officially banned with a morose Victoria being 'not amused' by all the frivolity! Parties, even unofficial ones, did however continue (even if covertly) and in an archive catalogue from 1891–92 one is able to see the breadth of choice for party organisers. Within a wide range of prices they could select designs such as Lilliputian crackers (4s 6d), Jewel crackers (4s 9d), Cupid's Playthings (7s), Somebody's Luggage (8s 6d), Fairytale crackers, Gypsy Queen and Mail Cart Luggage all at 10s 6d, Gems and Jewels and Mother Hubbard's at 14s, Lucky Box and Lovers' Secrets at 16s, Ally Soper's Trunk (18s), Tom Smith's Hat Box (20s), Box of Fun (21s), Darwinian crackers (24s), Bank of Love (27s), Mysterious crackers (30s), Dolly's Xmas Wardrobe (33s), Butterfly Ball (42s) and Bal Masque (48s).

Some of these prices appear rather high for the period but certainly they seem to have been based more on the quality of presentation and content rather than being exclusively aimed at the upper classes.

LEFT *Delightful Victorian graphics from the 1891–92 season are represented here in the Bal Masque (Masked Ball). A combination box of crackers and face masks in what was described as 'the perfect surprize.'*

RIGHT *The 1906–07 season offered yet another assortment of masks, hats, caps and bonnets – the designs of which were also reflected on the actual cracker scraps.*

However, it must be said that at the upper end of the range, it was probably only the upper classes that could afford them!

For those who didn't attend so many parties, Tom Smith's even catered for the unattached people of the day as they offered Crackers for Spinsters, Bachelors; for those who had already tied the knot, there were Crackers for Married Folk. Amusing novelties to be found within these crackers would include: wedding rings, keepers, faded flowers, night caps, thimbles, mirrors, shirt buttons, powder puffs, hair dye, kiss curls and tradesman's bills for spinsters; pipes, bottles of champagne, latchkeys, a candle and stick, a writ, pawn tickets, cigars, empty purses, tradesman's bills and a pack of cards for bachelors; and married couples were offered a candle and candlestick, sets of fire irons, cradles, feeding bottles, frying pans, flat irons, pipes, wedding rings and keepers.

A catalogue footnote to these products reflects how attitudes have changed out of all recognition from that time as the company, for some peculiar reason, felt constrained to add the warning 'not recommended for juveniles!'

Who within the company decided upon these rather eclectic contents is unknown but, whoever it was, it gives us today an amusing insight into what were considered to be 'essentials' to these three sectors of society. Or were they selected to be very much tongue in cheek?

There were many other fine novelties on offer, including the three-dimensional 'Love in a Cottage', Suitcases (trunks), Temple Bars, stand-up landscapes, pop-up kits to create an orchestra, and optical toys. Another example of Tom Smith's ability to keep up with the current trends and to add value to his products were 'Stereoscope' crackers whereby the actual box converted into a stereoscope which, after its original invention in 1838, was very popular in numerous Victorian homes. Many families had these viewers and millions of stereo cards were available for use with them. Much later, crackers relating to prize games were introduced featuring Snakes and Ladders and Ludo, for example. Also introduced was the Zillograph game which involved illustrations of faces that changed in expression, as well as crackers covering card games, the Klondyke Gold Rush, Egyptian treasure and many more. The product selection, in numerous sizes, seemed almost endless.

And, purely for selfish reasons, I cannot leave this section without mentioning the 1876 'Russian Luggage' which was described as:

New Costume Cosaques for Christmas, in new shaped trunks, with straps and lock, etc. each containing one dozen crackers, surmounted with Chromo Litho print of Russia under wintry aspect, the Duke and Duchess of Edinburgh sleighing in the vicinity of St Petersburg. One of the prettiest Cosaques yet designed. [Note how the word Cosaques is used here again.]

Among all the many designs on offer, Tom Smith's often, no doubt innocently, produced items that in today's litigious society would most certainly have got the company into some pretty hot water. Between the turn of the century and at least into the 1920s, boxes such as Sambo crackers, Darkies' Surprise, Darkies' Delight, Golliwog crackers and Coon crackers all regularly appeared along with other designs featuring illustrations of black folk in some situation or other. The Batger company also chipped in with its Black & White and Serenade crackers, the latter featuring a black minstrel offering up a ditty to a black woman on a balcony. Although not suited to today's sensibilities, these stereotypes simply reflected the general attitudes during the later Victorian period through to the 1920s and 1930s, as did many other products during those times and I am sure that in reality there was no intent.

Tom Smith's Cracker Box Designs

over the period
1891–1931

TOM SMITH & CO., 69, 67, and 65, Wilson Street, Finsbury, London, E.C.

Christmas Crackers—*continued*.

MASONIC CRACKERS. No. 564.

Of beautiful and appropriate design. One Dozen Crackers, resplendent in Purple and Gold, containing Masonic Aprons, Signs, Symbols, and amusing Emblems, with new and original " Mottoes" for Freemasons and others.

Per dozen boxes ...   .   **24 -**

YE OLDEN TIMES. No. 667.

A highly artistic Box of Crackers, being a representation of the Pompadour period, the general effect in a rich Azure Blue. Containing, in place of the usual Love Motto, an old English love verse, printed on paper of the olden style, together with a variety of old-fashioned Head-dresses. Packed in attractive Boxes, mounted with finely executed label, representing " Sweethearts of the Olden Time."

Per dozen boxes ...   . **24 -**

MUSICAL TOY CRACKERS. No. 510.

The greatest novelty for juveniles ever produced. In Twelve Crackers are found Twelve different Musical Toys, such as Bagpipes, Trumpets, Jews' Harps, Mouth Harmonicans, Mirlitons, and many other Musical Novelties. Made in Gelatine, with printed ends representing Music, and ornamented with pictures of Children. The Box, covered in Frosted Gold Paper, has an attractive label illustrating the contents.

Per dozen boxes ...   .   **24 -**

THE ENCHANTED BOX. No. 542.

A novel Box of Surprise Crackers, of superb and chaste design, containing many startling surprises, including Japanese Insects, Flexible Faces, Moustaches, Eye Glasses, Jewels, Bric-a-Brac, and Somebody's Luggage. One of the choicest and most amusing Boxes ever produced.

Per dozen boxes ...   . **24 -**

Tom Smith & Co. are also Manufacturers of Fine Confectionery.

26   TOM SMITH & Co., 69, 67 and 65, Wilson Street, Finsbury, London, E.C.

CHRISTMAS CRACKERS—*continued*.

TOM SMITH S PRIZE MODEL VIOLIN.
No. 3081.

Packed in the centre of the box, with twelve Musical Toy Crackers, is a model Violin and Bow of remarkable value. The person obtaining the Prize Ticket from one of the Crackers is entitled to the Violin.

Per dozen boxes ... 24-

CRACKERS FOR MARRIED FOLKS.
No. 256.

An amusing box for Married Folks, but not suitable for children. The Crackers are designed to represent the various phases in domestic life, and contain interesting articles such as Candle and Candlestick, Set of Fire Irons, Cradle, Feeding Bottle, Frying Pan, Flat Iron, Pipe, Wedding Ring and Keeper, and many other highly amusing Novelties, together with appropriate verses to each.

Per dozen boxes 24-

TOM SMITH'S MAGIC RAINBOW TOPS.
No. 3083.

Packed in the centre of the box of twelve brilliant Crackers are four Magic Tops, together with the spinner, by the use of which the four tops can be kept spinning at one time on the table. The Crackers contain a variety of Toys and one Prize Ticket. The person obtaining the Prize Ticket is entitled to the Magic Tops packed in the centre of the box.

Per dozen boxes ... 24-

GAME OF TICKET COLLECTORS.
No. 3082.

Immensely amusing for children. Arranged in the centre of the box, between the twelve Crackers, is the game of Ticket Collectors, which consists of Guard's Badge, Whistle, Ticket Punch, and Railway Tickets to various Towns. The Crackers contain a variety of Railway Hats, Caps, &c., and one Prize Ticket. The person obtaining the Prize Ticket is entitled to the game.

Per dozen boxes ... 24-

TOM SMITH'S HALF=CROWN BOX OF SURPRISE CRACKERS. No. 717.

A monster box containing 36 elegantly designed Crackers instead of the usual one dozen, as follows : 12 Crackers containing a variety of Hats, Caps and Bonnets, 12 Crackers containing a variety of miniature Toys, and 12 Crackers containing a variety of Gems and Jewels, with entirely original Love Mottoes. A marvel of cheapness.

Per dozen boxes ... 24/-

TOM SMITH & Co. are also Manufacturers of Fine Confectionery

By Royal Warrants.

CHRISTMAS CRACKERS—*continued.*

TOM SMITH'S JAPANESE NOVELTIES.
No. 692.

A monster box of Japanese Crackers, 14 inches long, made with Crimson and Orange Gelatine centres, ornamented with Miniature Fans, while the ends are of real Japanese Frilled Papers, spangled with Gold. The Crackers contain all the latest Novelties in real Japanese Toys and Curios, such as Vases, Jugs, Teapots, Fans, Insects, Reptiles, Umbrellas, etc., with Japanese Mottoes, and translation of same   Size of box, 14½ × 10 × 3¼ inches.

Per dozen boxes 36/-

TOM SMITH'S GRECIAN JEWELS.
No. 617.

A lovely box of Art Crackers made in Heliotrope Satin Gelatine with Golden Tinsel ends and decorated in the centres with Art Pictures of Grecian Women. The Crackers contain imitation Jewellery representing Diamonds, Sapphires, Emeralds, Turquoise, Rubies, Coral, etc., made in the form of Pins, Rings, Pendants, Brooches, Necklets, etc., together with Fortune Telling Jewel Mottoes.

Per dozen boxes 36/-

TOM SMITH'S COLLAPSIBLE HATS AND CAPS.   No. 541.

A highly-amusing box of brilliant Crackers, 14 inches long, containing Collapsible Hats and Caps of various designs, as illustrated on the Crackers, and causing roars of laughter when worn. The Crackers also contain Picture Puzzles in place of Mottoes.

Per dozen boxes 36/-

TOM SMITH'S ANIMATED INSECTS AND REPTILES.   No. 619.

Most novel and amusing. The Crackers contain Insects 3 or 4 inches long, with shaking legs and suspended from a thread; also Reptiles, such as Tortoises, Alligators, Snakes, etc., causing immense amusement to children and adults. The Crackers are made in Crimson and Forest Green with rich Gold fringed ends, and are decorated with Pictures of Tropical Insects and Reptiles. Size of box, 14½ × 9½ × 3 in.

Per dozen boxes, 12 Crackers in a box   ...   42/-
No. 620.   „   6   „   „   ...   21/-
See Coloured Plate R.

Tom Smith & Co., Ltd., are also Manufacturers of Fine Confectionery.

By Appointments to Their Majesties King George V. and Queen Mary.   35

CHRISTMAS CRACKERS—*continued.*

TOM SMITH'S FIRE BRIGADE CRACKERS. No. 530.

One of the most brilliant boxes ever produced. The Crackers are made in Crimson Gelatine and Gold Papers to produce a Fire Effect, and are decorated with Firemen in the exercise of their various duties. Inside the Crackers will be found Firemen's Hats and Helmets, Miniature Fire Engines, Extension Ladders, Squirts, etc., etc.

Per dozen boxes 33/-

HEROES OF THE EMPIRE. No. 252.

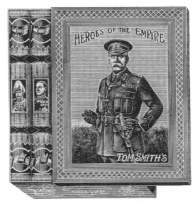

A brilliant box of Crimson Crackers, patriotic in design, decorated at the ends with representations of Allied Flags and in the centres with striking photos of Lord Kitchener, Admiral Jellicoe, Sir John French, Rear-Admiral C. E. Madden, etc. The contents of the Crackers are Head-dresses of Generals, Admirals, Naval Captains, Army Captains, Midshipmen, Naval Lieutenants, Army Lieutenants, and characteristic head-dresses of India and our Colonies. Each Cracker also contains a War Shooting Picture and a Patriotic Verse.

Per dozen boxes 36/-

See Coloured Plate R.

TOM SMITH'S ART CRACKERS. No. 167.

A charming box of artistic Crackers, designed in a lovely shade of Pink Gelatine with Gold ends, and decorated with Medallion Pictures of beautiful Women. The Crackers contain a splendid collection of Christmas Souvenirs, including Sprigs of Mistletoe, Bottles of Perfume, Forget-me-nots, Powder-Puffs, Robins, Scented Flowers, Pretty Pendants, Bracelets, Rings, Charms, etc., and many other Curios, together with appropriate Verses.

Per dozen boxes 36/-

BRIC-A-BRAC CRACKERS. No. 514.

Owing to the immense popularity of these Crackers, an elaborate revival embracing a large variety of contents is here presented. The box is decorated on the top and four sides with a set of very charming designs, executed in the highest style of chromo-lithography, and represents the contents of the Crackers, which include charming little Curios, Bric-a-Brac, and *Articles de Vertu*, such as Miniature Terra-Cotta Figures, Japanese Figures, Fans, Screens, China Pug Dogs, etc.

Per dozen boxes 36/-

Tom Smith & Co., Ltd., are also Manufacturers of Fine Confectionery.

Tom Smith & Co., Ltd., Wilson Street, Finsbury Square, London, E.C. 2.   21

CHRISTMAS CRACKERS—*continued.*

DARKIES' SURPRISE. No. 924.

A box of Tropical Crackers in Crimson Crepe paper, ornamented with Niggers and Sailors. The Crackers contain Nigger Figures, Lucky Black Baby, miniature Warships and Submarines, Necklaces, Bracelets, Anchors and a Sailor's Cap, together with Optical Puzzles.

Per dozen boxes 40/-

Parcelled in Quarter-dozens.

See Coloured Plate P.

TOM SMITH'S DESERT CRACKERS.
No. 926.

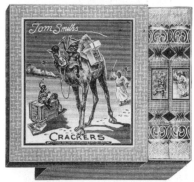

Made in Orange Gelatine and Yellow Crepe papers, and ornamented with Black Boys and Arabs. The Crackers contain Camels, Aeroplanes, Sphinx Figures, Sheik's Hat, Turk's Hat, Pitchers and other novelties in connection with the desert, with Riddles in place of Mottoes.

Per dozen boxes 42/-

Parcelled in Quarter-dozens.   *See Coloured Plate O.*

WHIRLIGIG CARNIVAL CRACKERS.
No. 738.

A brilliant box of Orange Gelatine Crackers, decorated with Carnival Figures, and containing Butterfly Ticklers, Garlands, Noses, Love Streamers, Balloons, Carnival Hats and Heads, together with up-to-date Skits.

Per dozen boxes 40/-

Parcelled in Quarter-dozens.

See Coloured Plate Q.

OUR CHARMING PRINCE. No. 745.

The Crackers are made in Crimson Gelatine and are ornamented with real little photos of our Charming Prince in four different attitudes. The crackers contain miniature Stirrups and Racing Horses, Motor Cars, Cigarettes, Captain's and First Officer's Hats, Jockey Cap, miniature Bust of H.R.H., etc., with specially composed verses.

SPECIMEN VERSE.
In hurdle race or steeplechase,
Tho' he can't always win it,
He rides with grace and makes the pace,
He's generally in it.

Per dozen boxes 42/-

Parcelled in Quarter-dozens.

Tom Smith & Co., Ltd., are also Manufacturers of Fine Confectionery.

Tom Smith & Co., Ltd., Wilson Street, Finsbury Square, London, E.C. 2.   27

CHRISTMAS CRACKERS—*continued.*

JILL IN THE BOX. No. 233.

The Crackers are made in brilliant Crimson Gelatine with Crimson, Black and Silver ends. They contain a good assortment of attractive Hats, Caps, Bonnets, Musical and other Toys, Curios, Jewels, with Quips and Jokes

Per dozen boxes 48/-

See Coloured Plate P.

FRIVOLITY CRACKERS. No. 127.

The Crackers contain Carnival Novelties, Dominos, Staring Eyes, Figures, Balloons, etc., with Quips, Jokes and clever Song Titles. The Crackers are in brilliant Orange and Crimson Gelatines ornamented with Pictures of Pierrot, his Lady Love and Jester.

Per dozen boxes 48/-

See Coloured Plate P.

TOM SMITH'S HATS, CAPS & BONNETS. No. 177.

The Crackers are in Orange Gelatine with Black, Silver and Gold ends. An assortment of attractive Hats, Caps and Bonnets will be found inside, together with Love Verses.

Per dozen boxes 48/-

"ALL SPORTS" CRACKERS. No. 856.

The Crackers are designed in Orange Gelatine, suitably decorated, and contain miniature Skis, Tennis Racquets, Hockey Sticks, Motor Cars, Golfing and Cricket Figures, etc., together with specially composed Sports Verses.

SPECIMEN VERSE.
I'm not the sort to miss a *catch*,
As you will soon discover.
I don't intend to lose the *match*,
You've bowled this *maiden over*.

Per dozen boxes 48/-

Tom Smith & Co., Ltd., are also Manufacturers of Fine Confectionery.

Tom Smith & Co., Ltd., Wilson Street, Finsbury Square, London, E.C. 2.   87

CHRISTMAS CRACKERS—*continued.*

HEAD-DRESSES, OLD AND NEW.
No. 242.

Tom Smith & Co. have endeavoured as far as possible to carry out the title in the contents of this box. Some of the Head-dresses portrayed on the lid, together with Curios and Jewels, will be found in the Crackers which are designed in Orange Gelatine, with Gold, Black and White ends.

Per dozen boxes 66/-

TOM SMITH'S XMAS PARTY. No. 942.

A thoroughly up-to-date box of Crimson and Gold Crackers, containing miniature Xmas Trees, Candelabra, Decanters, Pianos, also Brooches, Musical Champagne Bottle, Moustaches, Love's Thermometer, etc., etc. Each Cracker also contains in addition an attractive Head-dress, with a Riddle or Optical Puzzle.

Per dozen boxes 66/-

QUARTETTE OF MIRTH.
No. 867.

A brilliant box of Crimson Gelatine Crackers, containing Streamers, Domino Masks, Trumpets, Balloons, Feather Darts, Noses, etc. and in addition each Cracker contains an attractive Hat, Cap or Bonnet, with Quips and Jokes.

Per dozen boxes 66/-

TOM SMITH'S CRACKER DANCE. No. 294.

A box of brilliant Crackers in Crimson Gelatine edged with Silver Bands and ornamented with Carnival Characters. The contents include Balloon, Candles, Powder Puff, miniature Bottle of Perfume, Champagne Bottle, Wine Glasses, Pack of Cards, Glass Slipper, and in addition each Cracker contains an artistic Hat, Cap or Bonnet, with an Acrostic Puzzle.

Per dozen boxes 68/-
See Coloured Plate R.

Tom Smith & Co., Ltd., are also Manufacturers of Fine Confectionery.

A SELECTION OF
TOM SMITH'S
NOVELTIES
FROM THE PERIOD
1906–1931

TOM SMITH & Co., 69, 67 and 65, Wilson Street, Finsbury, London, E.C.

NOVELTIES—*continued.*
FILLED WITH FONDANTS, CHOCOLATES, &c.
NOTE—All Nos. having the letter "C" affixed, denotes the article is filled with Chocolates.

No. 842c    No. 843c    No. 845c    No. 386c

No.		Per doz.
860c	House Boat, prettily painted model, clockwork, size 6×3	13 6
842c	Motor Car, latest design, enamelled in colours and gilt, clockwork, size 8½×4½	13 9
843c	Kennel Money Box, in dark oak wood, "Poker Work" decoration, lock and key, size 7×4×4	13 9
844	Miniature Wall Cupboard, in dark stained wood, size 10×3½×2½	13 9

No.		Per doz
76	Secret Money Cabinet, with gilt handle, corners, etc., lock and key, size 5¾×3¼	14/
386c	Tea Pot, imitation "Wedgwood" china, size 6½×3¾	14/
692c	Motor Car, latest novelty in clockwork, prettily finished, size 7×4	14/
845c	Cat and Mouse Trap, clockwork, amusing toy (see coloured illustration), size 8×6	14/

No. 846 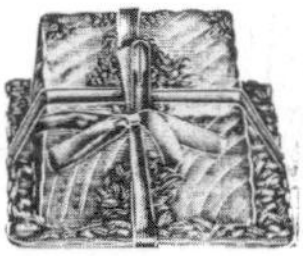   No. 847    No. 681c    No. 848    No. 850

No.		Per doz.
681c	Ladies' Wrist Bag, nickel chain and mounts, size 6½×4½	14/
846	"Seat" Money Cabinet, oak wood, with tray inside, bright metal fittings, lock and key, size 5×3½×3½	14/
847	Cheese Dish, China, with floral and gilt decoration (see coloured illustration), size 6×5×2¾	14/
848	Sardine Dish, China, floral and gilt decoration (see coloured illustration), size 6¼×5×3	14/

No.		Per doz
850	Smokers' Cabinet in oak wood, with ash tray and match-box holder, metal corners, useful present, size 8½×4½×2	14/
851	Sardine Dish, China, as No. 848, size 7×5½×3½	18/
852	Work Box, imitation leather, fitted with silks, cottons, etc., size 6×4½×2¾	18/

No. 853c    No. 696    No. 854c

No.		Per doz.
691	Oak Cabinet, decorated with metal fittings, artistic shape, lock and key, size 6½×4½×3¾	22/6
853c	The "Favourite" Tea Set, floral and gilt decoration on white china, consisting of tea pot (3¾ in. high), jug and basin, two cups and saucers ... per doz. sets	22/6

No.		Per doz
851c	Railway Engine, perfect model of G.N.R. or M. Ry., special strong clockwork action with bell (see coloured illustration), size 9×4½×2¼	24

No. 856c   No. 691   No. 859c

No.		Per doz.
856c	Fire Engine, well made model, with clockwork action, size 10×5	24/
695c	Japanese "Kaga" China Tea Set, consisting of tea pot, cream jug, basin, and two cups and saucers	42/

No.		Per doz
859c	The "Rose" Tea Set, in white china, with rose and leaf decoration, consisting of tea pot (4½×5), jug and basin, 2 cups and saucers, most acceptable present ... per doz. sets	36/
695	Oak Wood Jewel Cabinet, fitted with divisions and drawer, lined plush, bright metal fittings, lock and key, size 8½×5½×3½	48/

Sole Proprietors of Tom Smith's Celebrated Christmas Crackers.

Tom Smith & Co., Ltd., Wilson Street, Finsbury Square, London, E.C. 2.   39

NOVELTIES—*continued*.

FILLED WITH PURE CONFECTIONERY, CHOCOLATES, &c.

NOTE.—All Nos. having the letter "C" affixed denotes the article is filled with Chocolates.

No. 705C.
10/6 per doz.
Wood Laundry Set.
Size 6 × 3½

No. 475C. **12/** per doz.
Metal Cash Box.
(Lock and Key.)
Size 5 × 3.

No. 712C. **12/** per doz.
Jap. China Cup & Saucer.
Green Decoration.
Size of Cup, 2¾ in. diam.

No. 713C. **12/** per doz
Jap. China Jug & Basin.
Green Decoration.
Size 4 × 3½

No. 406C.
12/6 per doz.
Metal Knife Grinder.
Size 4½ in. high.

No. 810C. **12/6** per doz.
Metal Locomotive (Clockwork).
Size 6 × 3½

No. 709C. **13/** per doz.
Robin and Fence.
Size 7 × 5.

No. 407C. **14/** per doz.
Metal Motor Boat (Clockwork).
Size 6¾ × 2.

No. 521C. **16/** per doz.
Jap. China Cup and Saucer.
Size of Cup, 3¾ in. diam.

No. 811C. **16/** per doz.
Metal Motor Cycle and Side Car
(Clockwork). Size 6 × 4.

No. 118C.
16/ per doz.
Size of Cup, 4 × 3

No. 420C. **28/** per doz.
China Teapot. Rosebud Design.
Size 7 × 3½

No. 419C.
16/ per doz.
Size 3½ × 3½

No. 708C. **16/** per doz.
Fancy Coloured Straw Basket.
Size 8 × 4.

No. 714C. **16/** per doz.
Jap. China Teapot.
Green Decoration.
Size 5 × 4.

No. 520C. **16/** per doz.
Metal Motor Car
(Mechanical).
Size 8 × 3½

No. 732. **16/** per doz.
Tom Smith's Market Basket.
containing an assortment of
Novelties. Size 7½ × 6.

No. 716C. **22/** per doz.
China Cup, Saucer & Plate.
Floral Decoration.
Size of Plate, 6½ in. diam.

No. 717C. **22/** per doz.
China "Crinoline Lady"
Powder Box.
Size 5½ in. high.

No. 525C. **22/6** per doz.
Metal Road Roller
(Clockwork).
Size 7 × 4½

No. 411C. **24/** per doz.
Metal Motor Car
(Mechanical).
Size 8 × 3½

No. 730. **18/** per doz.
Tambourine, containing assortment
of Novelties. Size 6¾ in. diam.
No. 731. Size 7¾ in. diam. **27/** per doz.

Sole Proprietors of Tom Smith's Celebrated Christmas Crackers.

NOVELTIES—*continued.*

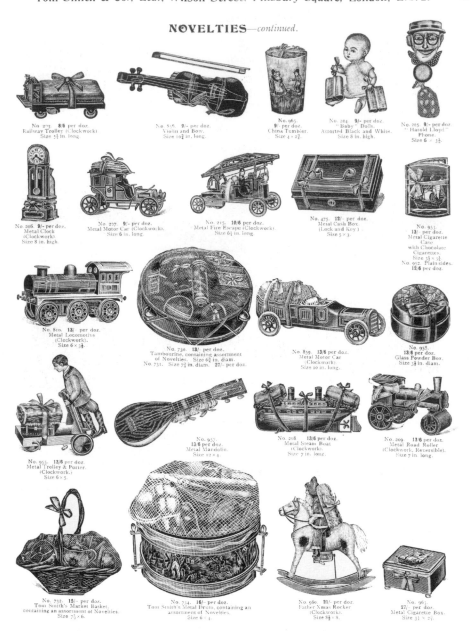

No. 203. **8/6** per doz.
Railway Trolley (Clockwork)
Size 4½ in. long

No. 836. **9/-** per doz.
Violin and Bow.
Size 10¾ in. long.

No. 965.
9/- per doz.
China Tumbler.
Size 4 × 2¾.

No. 204. **9/-** per doz.
"Baby" Dolls.
Assorted Black and White.
Size 8 in. high.

No. 205. **9/-** per doz.
" Harold Lloyd "
Phone.
Size 6 × 3½.

No. 206. **9/-** per doz.
Metal Clock
(Clockwork)
Size 8 in. high.

No. 227. **9/-** per doz.
Metal Motor Car (Clockwork).
Size 6 in. long.

No. 215. **10/6** per doz.
Metal Fire Escape (Clockwork).
Size 6½ in. long.

No. 475. **12/-** per doz.
Metal Cash Box.
(Lock and Key).
Size 5 × 3.

No. 953.
13/- per doz.
Metal Cigarette
Case
with Chocolate
Cigarettes.
Size 3½ × 3½.
No. 952. Plain sides.
12/6 per doz.

No. 810. **13/-** per doz.
Metal Locomotive
(Clockwork).
Size 6 × 3½.

No. 730. **13/-** per doz.
Tambourine, containing assortment
of Novelties. Size 6½ in. diam.
No. 731. Size 7½ in. diam. **27/-** per doz.

No. 859. **13/6** per doz.
Metal Motor Car
(Clockwork)
Size 10 in. long.

No. 958.
13/6 per doz.
Glass Powder Box.
Size 3½ in. diam.

No. 955. **13/6** per doz.
Metal Trolley & Porter.
(Clockwork.)
Size 6 × 5.

No. 957.
13/6 per doz.
Metal Mandolin.
Size 12 × 4.

No. 208. **13/6** per doz.
Metal Steam Boat
(Clockwork).
Size 7 in. long.

No. 209. **13/6** per doz.
Metal Road Roller
(Clockwork, Reversible).
Size 7 in. long.

No. 732. **15/-** per doz.
Tom Smith's Market Basket,
containing an assortment of Novelties.
Size 7½ × 6.

No. 734. **16/-** per doz.
Tom Smith's Metal Drum, containing an
assortment of Novelties.
Size 6 × 4.

No. 960. **21/-** per doz.
Father Xmas Rocker
(Clockwork).
Size 8½ × 8.

No. 963.
27/- per doz.
Metal Cigarette Box.
Size 3½ × 2½.

Sole Proprietors of Tom Smith's Celebrated Christmas Crackers.

Tom Smith & Co., Ltd., Wilson Street, Finsbury Square, London, E.C. 2.

NOVELTIES—*continued.*

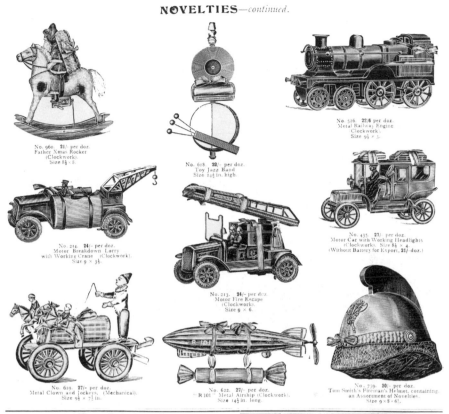

No. 960. **21/-** per doz.
Father Xmas Rocker
(Clockwork).
Size 8½ × 8.

No. 618. **22/-** per doz.
Toy Jazz Band
Size 14½ in. high.

No. 526. **22/6** per doz.
Metal Railway Engine
(Clockwork).
Size 9½ × 3.

No. 214. **24/-** per doz.
Motor Breakdown Lorry
with Working Crane (Clockwork).
Size 9 × 3½.

No. 213. **24/-** per doz.
Motor Fire Escape
(Clockwork).
Size 9 × 6.

No. 435. **27/-** per doz.
Motor Car with Working Headlights
(Clockwork). Size 8½ × 4.
(Without Battery for Export, 21/- doz.)

No. 619. **27/-** per doz.
Metal Clown and Jockeys. (Mechanical).
Size 9½ × 7½ in.

No. 622. **27/-** per doz.
"R 101" Metal Airship (Clockwork).
Size 14½ in. long.

No. 739. **30/-** per doz.
Tom Smith's Fireman's Helmet, containing
an Assortment of Novelties.
Size 9 × 8 - 6½.

IMITATION CHRISTMAS TREES.

Xmas Trees in Wooden
Stands

No.			per doz.
700	Size 16 in. high	...	**4/6**
701	,, 25 ,, ,,	...	**8/6**
702	,, 32 ,, ,,	...	**18/-**
703	,, 39 ,, ,,	...	**24/-**
704	,, 40 ,, ,,	...	**30/-**
705	,, 48 ,, ,,	...	**48/-**
706	Miniature Tree with Candles on Card Box, size 6¾ in. high		**6/-**

IMITATION STAINED GLASS LANTERNS.

MADE TO FOLD PERFECTLY FLAT.

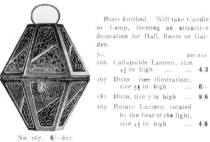

No. 167. **6/-** doz.

Brass finished. Will take Candle
or Lamp, forming an attractive
decoration for Hall, Room or Garden.

No.			per doz.
166	Collapsible Lantern, size 4½ in. high	... ...	**4/3**
167	Ditto (see illustration), size 5½ in. high	...	**6/-**
181	Ditto, size 7 in. high	...	**8/6**
165	Rotary Lantern, rotated by the heat of the light, size 4½ in. high	...	**4/6**

Sole Proprietors of Tom Smith's Celebrated Christmas Crackers.

OTHER ATTRACTIONS

Allied to his cracker business, Tom Smith also stocked and sold numerous decorative festive items. To name but a few, the selection included: Christmas decorations; candle ornaments; hanging grape bunches; napkin bouquets; holly wreaths; glazed vine leaves; magic flowers; dessert and fish papers; flags and banners; French satin boxes; Christmas figures, birds and lanterns.

For the discerning shopkeeper, there were cottages, windmills, trains, clocks, pies and water mills, all displayed under glass domes. Similarly for window displays, confectioners could purchase automatons in the form of dancing sailors, Paddy's obstinate pig, Darwinian cooks and mechanical tea drinkers.

The years 1895-96 saw the company offering 'Window Attractions – Musical & Mechanical Of The Finest French Manufacture' and very fine they were, with the Parisian laundress, Japanese tea drinker, singing cook, seated figure with baton and music, Chinaman, and Negro being among the best.

To supplement all this, one could further obtain clockwork pictures, with or without music and costing between 17s and 25s. Musical versions would run for about one hour when fully wound. Subject matter included a woman with cat, man and rat, children with a jack-in-the-box, children with dog, dog's concert, ballet dancer and chicks, and dancing lesson.

To cap it all, you could acquire the strangely named 'Tom Smith's Relics from Pompeii' – a range of imitation artefacts, which the catalogue describes as 'the most remarkable novelties ever produced, consisting of daggers, padlocks, caskets etc., made to imitate old iron to such perfection as to render detection almost impossible'. However, the imitation daggers would certainly not go down too well with the forces of law and order in today's society!

FIREWORK FUN

While in the main this book concentrates on the story of the Christmas cracker with its conventional contents, one should not forget that over a great many years, even as far back as the early 1880s and probably even before then, Tom Smith's were offering boxes of crackers filled with what we today call indoor fireworks.

In more recent times, these little fireworks were not so much contained inside actual crackers, but were marketed more on the basis of small self-contained ranges in their own right, whereby specialised 'pyrotechnic' selections of little tablets, matches or sparklers were attached to amusing brightly coloured picture cards – to be ignited on a saucer or plate after the Christmas meal.

I well remember, during my time with the company in Norwich, seeing the team of girls (working in a sort of safe house known as the 'Firework Department') surrounded by piles of sparklers, Bengal matches, coloured aspirin-like tablets and tubes laboriously sticking these little fireworks onto their display cards. It was a rather slow method and one that probably hadn't changed much for well over 100 years, but production speeds were greatly improved by the introduction of the more modern blister-packing method (and no glue!) in around 1990.

LEFT *From 1928–29, we have a superb design for 'Firework Crackers' with the assembled crowd enjoying a glittering firework display in front of the world-famous Crystal Palace.*

RIGHT *This fine 1910–11 box of 'Parlour Fireworks' features a group of excited children having fun with crackers and indoor fireworks.*

The offerings of the 1980s and 1990s were marketed as 'Indoor Fireworks' in their own right and for Halloween, there was the 'Midnight' range featuring such spooky names to conjure with as Giant Cobra, Serpents of Doom, Wizard's Wands, Bat's Breath, Swamp Fires, Midnight Flares, Witches Brew and Magic Dust.

However, back in Victorian and Edwardian times, and even into the reign of George V, these little amusements were usually referred to as 'Parlour' fireworks (with, as ever, super graphics) – a name that, more in keeping with those times, seemed to suggest much more of a family 'togetherness', which in fact was probably more the way it was anyway.

CHAPTER FOUR

MOTTOS & VERSES

Questions are often asked about the mottos traditionally contained within each cracker. While in the early days each motto was very specifically linked to some type of loving verse or occasion, the situation has changed somewhat today and the motto now covers such things as general knowledge, quizzes, facts and figures, puzzles, basic corny jokes and numerous subjects and devices to create a few minutes' fun at the festive table.

Taken from an early catalogue, the following is an example of a typical love motto or 'love proverb' as the company called them, originally used in connection with Tom Smith's 'Christmas Proverb Crackers':

STOLEN KISSES ARE ALWAYS THE SWEETEST

> *They lingered long as the twilight fell,*
> *Away from the haunts of men,*
> *There was no one there to tell the tale,*
> *So he kissed her once again;*
> *Said he – 'My love, this furtive tryst,*
> *Is the sweetest man e'er knew,*
> *And the maid's eyes smiled through the even's mist,*
> *As she said – 'The proverb's true.'*

What did the waste
paper basket say
to the bin?

Oh, stop talking rubbish!

What did Paddington
and Winnie the Pooh
take on holiday?

Just the bear essentials!

Why did the woodman
spare the trees?

*Because he was a
good fella!*

What did the sink say
to the leaking tap?

*Stop being such
a drip!*

What's the oldest
fruit of all?

Elderberries!

When is a Christmas
pudding musical?

When it's piping hot!

What do butterflies
sleep on?

Caterpillows!

What do solicitors
wear to work?

Law suits!

How do you keep
sheep warm in winter?

By central bleating!

Why did the banana
go out with the prune?

*Because it couldn't
find a date!*

What must you know
to be an auctioneer?

Lots!

Did you hear about the
couple who lived in
a lighthouse?

*Their marriage was said
to be on the rocks!*

How do rabbits
make beer?

*I think they start
with the hops!*

What is a lawyer's
favourite pudding?

Sue-it!

What do you get
if you cross a banana
with a rug?

Carpet slippers!

Gone are the days of the early florid love mottos. Here we have twenty-first-century offerings – much more reliant upon the corny joke. These examples were kindly supplied by Upper Crust Crackers.

The 1875 catalogue in its 'Various Novelties and Surprises' section – under Floral Cosaques – offers:

FAIRIES USE FLOWERS FOR THEIR CHARACTERY
Shakespeare

Oh! Flowers, sweet flowers, the fairest gems that Earth,
Upon her bounteous bosom, loves to cherish,
Bright, yet as pure as childhood's thoughtless mirth,
Although like morning dreams, they quickly perish.

By them the lover tells his silent tail,
They can by every hope and fear express,
The mind, when words and looks would surely fail,
Can thus a secret charmingly confess.

Yet another offering in 'Under The Mistletoe' tells us:

KISSING CRACKERS – THE SWEETEST OF ALL CHRISTMAS BON-BONS.

Jack O'Dandy, show yourself handy
At something sweeter than sugar candy
You are not often guilty of very great folly
Go you MUST, snatch a kiss from pretty Polly.

And to leave the potential purchaser in no doubt, it advises that 'The crackers are assorted in the boxes, those with red ends being for the ladies, and those with green ends for the gentlemen.' Note, also, how these 'Kissing Crackers' are also referred to as 'Bon-Bons' at this time.

Similarly, many other mottos were linked with a wide range of subjects from sports, topical events or pastimes. Typical specimen verse examples read:

PETER PAN CRACKERS

Joy's donor with his fairy spell,
Dear Peter Pan can be:
But you could do it just as well
With one sweet word – for me.

FOOTBALL CRACKERS

From ease and comfort I would part,
Yes, with a glad ungrudging soul
And make a football of my heart,
If you would 'Kick' it into 'Goal'.

GOLFING CRACKERS

If I played Golf with you, I fear,
I'd fail to 'Score' the whole game thro';
My heart is perforated dear,
And all the 'Holes' are made by you.

BRIDGE PARTY CRACKERS

I draw the line at Bridge divine,
And this is why and wherefore,
The Draw-Bridge of your Heart to mine,
Is th' only Bridge I care for!

HIGH LIFE CRACKERS

A cheek more dainty than the peach,
Lips rosier than the rose to kiss;
Is 'High life' high enough to reach,
To such a Heaven as this?

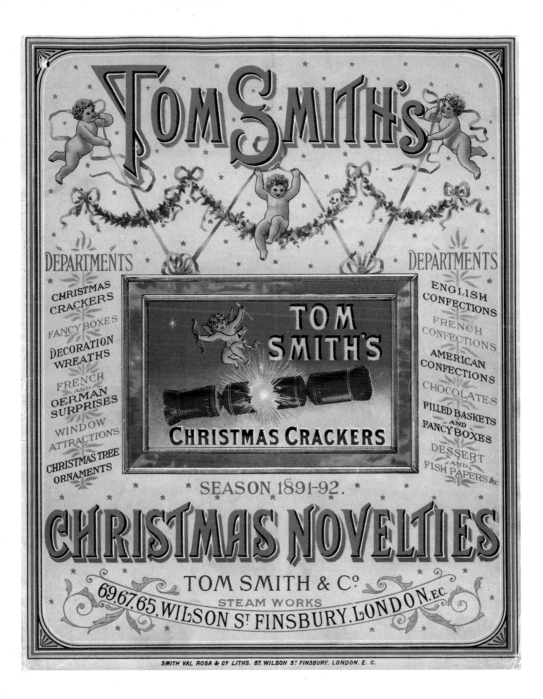

The stunning front cover of the 1891–92 catalogue printed by the Smith Val Rosa company in London, which indicated the company's vast range of products on offer at that time.

TOP *Beautiful crackers and a wonderful 'Court Jester'. This super graphic appeared in the early years of George V's reign.*

ABOVE *Slightly seductive, slightly romantic, 'Rouge et Noir' offers a French touch to this fine Edwardian design.*

PLATE R.

TOM SMITH'S SPECIAL BOX ASSORTED CRACKERS. No. 380.

Per Dozen Boxes, 24/-

TOM SMITH'S CRACKERS OF ALL NATIONS No. 382.

Per Dozen Boxes, 27/-

SECRETS OF THE TOILET. No. 384.

Per Dozen Boxes, 30/-

TOM SMITH'S POMPEIAN ART CRACKERS. No. 387

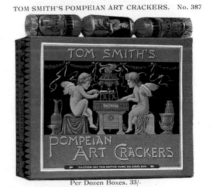

Per Dozen Boxes, 33/-

SIGNS OF THE TIMES CRACKERS. No. 385.

Per Dozen Boxes, 33/-

TOM SMITH'S ART NOUVEAU JEWEL CRACKERS. No. 389.

Per Dozen Boxes, 39/-

TOM SMITH & Co., 69, 67 and 65, Wilson Street, Finsbury, London, E.C.

Six excellent box designs from 1906–07 featuring superb and typical graphics of the period with the art nouveau lady at the bottom right being a particularly nice example.

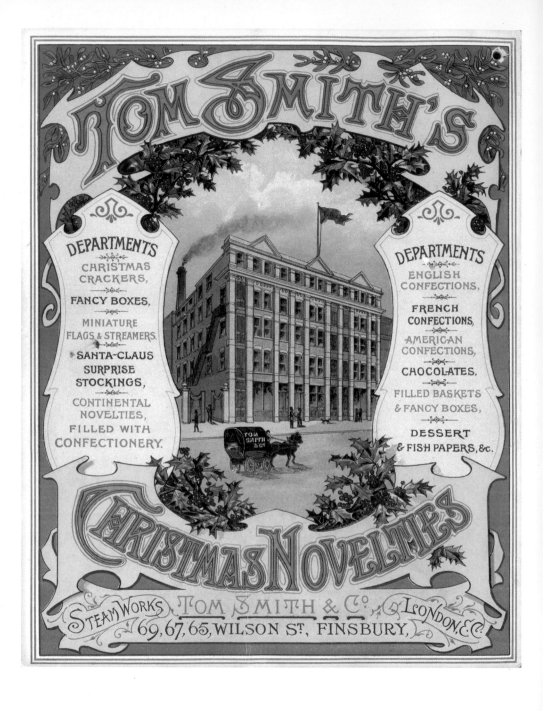

A must for inclusion! The reverse cover of the previous page showing an excellent graphic interpretation of Smith's Wilson Street factory in Finsbury, London. Wilson Street itself still exists today.

PLATE P.

TOM SMITH'S 1/6 BOX
ANGLO-FRENCH CRACKERS.
No. 366.

Per Dozen Boxes, 12/6

TOM SMITH'S
MUSICAL TOY CRACKERS.
No 369.

Per Dozen Boxes, 15/-

PUZZLES FOR THE
POSTMAN.
No. 370.

Per Dozen Boxes, 16/-

TOM SMITH'S
FOOTBALL CRACKERS. No. 372.

Per Dozen Boxes, 18/-

CAPE TO CAIRO
CRACKERS.
No. 373.

Per Dozen Boxes, 18/-

TOM SMITH'S
SPECIAL COSTUME BOX. No. 293.

Per Dozen Boxes, 18/-

CHRISTMAS PARTY CRACKERS.
No. 374.

Per Dozen Boxes, 20/-

TOM SMITH'S MOUNT VESUVIUS CRACKERS.   No 378.

Per Dozen Boxes, 22/-

TOM SMITH & Co., 69, 67 and 65, Wilson Street, Finsbury, London, E.C.

*Cracker boxes from the cheaper to middle end of the market are featured on this page from the company's
1906–07 catalogue.*

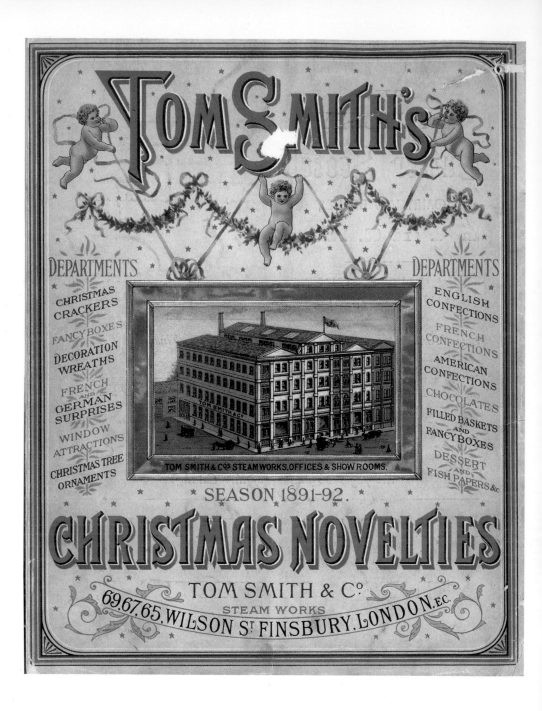

The slight damage does not detract from this fine reverse cover of the image on the previous page – again from the 1891–92 catalogue. I always wanted to know what cherubs did for a living!

Another front cover, this time from the 1906–07 edition of the company catalogue, featuring a cracker-laden Santa and again listing the company's diverse range.

The mask has been removed, the cracker pulled and our romantic clown gets down to the serious business of serenading the lady as seen in this 'Joie de Vivre' design, probably produced in the 1920s and showing all the usual Tom Smith's flair. By kind permission of Diane Fellas.

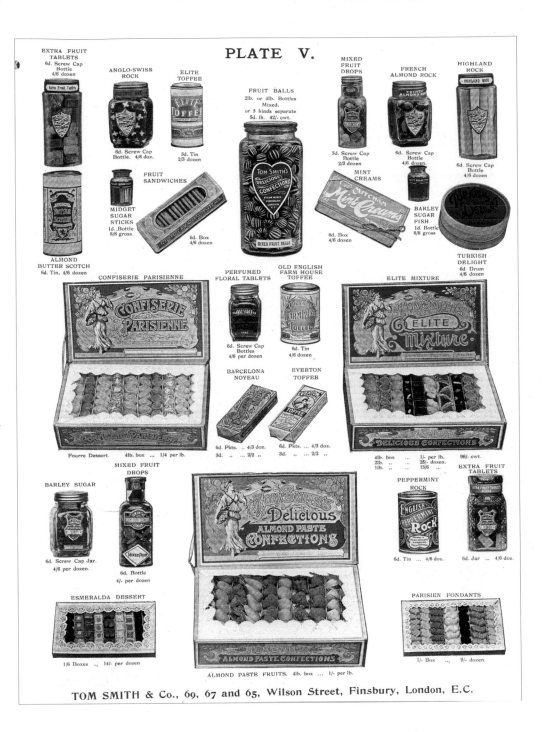

PLATE V.

EXTRA FRUIT TABLETS
6d. Screw Cap Bottle
4/6 dozen

ANGLO-SWISS ROCK
6d. Screw Cap Bottle. 4/6 doz.

ELITE TOFFEE
3d. Tin 2/3 dozen

FRUIT BALLS
2lb. or 4lb. Bottles Mixed, or 5 kinds separate
5d. lb. 42/- cwt.

MIXED FRUIT DROPS
3d. Screw Cap Bottle 2/3 dozen

FRENCH ALMOND ROCK
6d. Screw Cap Bottle 4/6 dozen

HIGHLAND ROCK
6d. Screw Cap Bottle 4/6 dozen

FRUIT SANDWICHES
6d. Box 4/6 dozen

MIDGET SUGAR STICKS
1d. Bottle 8/8 gross.

MINT CREAMS
6d. Box 4/6 dozen

BARLEY SUGAR FISH
1d. Bottle 8/8 gross

ALMOND BUTTER SCOTCH
6d. Tin, 4/6 dozen

TURKISH DELIGHT
6d Drum 4/6 dozen

CONFISERIE PARISIENNE
Fourre Dessert. 4lb. box ... 1/4 per lb.

PERFUMED FLORAL TABLETS
6d. Screw Cap Bottles 4/6 per dozen

OLD ENGLISH FARM HOUSE TOFFEE
6d. Tin 4/6 dozen

ELITE MIXTURE
4lb. box ... 1/- per lb.
2lb. ,, ... 25/- dozen.
1lb. ,, ... 13/6 ,,
96/- cwt.

BARCELONA NOYEAU
6d. Pkts. .. 4/3 doz.
3d. ,, .. 2/2 ,,

EVERTON TOFFEE
6d. Pkts. ... 4/3 doz.
3d. ,, ... 2/2 ,,

BARLEY SUGAR
6d. Screw Cap Jar. 4/6 per dozen.

MIXED FRUIT DROPS
6d. Bottle 4/- per dozen

ALMOND PASTE FRUITS. 4lb. box ... 1/- per lb.

PEPPERMINT ROCK
6d. Tin ... 4/6 doz.

EXTRA FRUIT TABLETS
6d. Jar ... 4/6 doz.

ESMERALDA DESSERT
1/6 Boxes .., 14/- per dozen.

PARISIEN FONDANTS
1/- Box .., 9/- dozen.

TOM SMITH & Co., 69, 67 and 65, Wilson Street, Finsbury, London, E.C.

Just a small selection of confectionery items that the company was offering in the early years of the twentieth century.

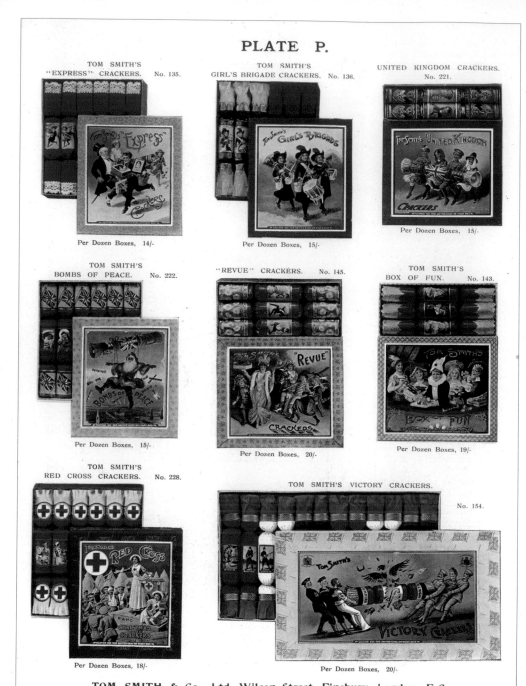

PLATE P.

TOM SMITH'S "EXPRESS" CRACKERS. No. 135.

Per Dozen Boxes, 14/-

TOM SMITH'S GIRL'S BRIGADE CRACKERS. No. 136.

Per Dozen Boxes, 15/-

UNITED KINGDOM CRACKERS. No. 221.

Per Dozen Boxes, 15/-

TOM SMITH'S BOMBS OF PEACE. No. 222.

Per Dozen Boxes, 15/-

"REVUE" CRACKERS. No. 145.

Per Dozen Boxes, 20/-

TOM SMITH'S BOX OF FUN. No. 143.

Per Dozen Boxes, 19/-

TOM SMITH'S RED CROSS CRACKERS. No. 228.

Per Dozen Boxes, 18/-

TOM SMITH'S VICTORY CRACKERS. No. 154.

Per Dozen Boxes, 20/-

TOM SMITH & Co., Ltd. Wilson Street, Finsbury, London, E.C.

Eight boxes from the 1917 catalogue during the First World War. Notice numbers 154, 222 and 228 all referring in one way or another to the conflict.

THE GREAT WAR!!
HOW
IT AFFECTS THE
CHRISTMAS TRADE.

The Stoppage of the Continental Supplies
of CHILDREN'S TOYS for Christmas
is sure to create an increased demand for

TOM SMITH'S
CHRISTMAS CRACKERS.
& SANTA CLAUS STOCKINGS.

A Huge Supply at popular Prices.

ALL BRITISH MADE.

Numerous Patriotic Novelties in all departments.
ORDERS SHOULD BE PLACED AT THE EARLIEST POSSIBLE DATE
OWING TO LIMITED SUPPLY OF MATERIAL.

TOM SMITH'S
DELICIOUS CONFECTIONS.
HIGHEST GRADE GOODS AT LOWEST MARKET PRICES.

Steam Works, Offices & Show Rooms.
WILSON STREET FINSBURY SQUARE LONDON E.C.

TELEGRAPHIC ADDRESS "CONFECTION LONDON."   TELEPHONE Nº LONDON WALL 1177.

*In 1917 things were getting a bit more difficult with various shortages. Nevertheless, the company was still
plugging away as seen with this product leaflet.*

TOM SMITH'S ARTISTIC CRACKERS FOR TABLE DECORATION.
ORIGINAL DESIGNS.

2373
24/- per doz. boxes.
6 in a box.

2356
24/- per doz. boxes.
12 in a box.

2359
24/- per doz. boxes.
12 in a box.

2377
27/- per doz. boxes.
6 in a box.

2350
16/- per doz. boxes.
12 in a box.

2358
24/- per doz. boxes.
12 in a box.

2372
21/- per doz. boxes.
6 in a box.

2381
33/- per doz. boxes.
6 in a box.

2374
24/- per doz. boxes.
6 in a box.

2380
33/- per doz. boxes.
6 in a box.

2378
30/- per doz. boxes.
6 in a box.

2370
18/- per doz. boxes.
6 in a box.

2376
27/- per doz. boxes.
6 in a box.

2355
21/- per doz. boxes.
12 in a box.

2379
30/- per doz. boxes.
6 in a box.

2357
24/- per doz. boxes.
12 in a box.

2382
36/- per doz. boxes
6 in a box.

TOM SMITH & Co., Ltd., Wilson Street, Finsbury, London, E.C.

A year or two before the First World War, Smith's was still offering amazing table decoration creations. Not quite so many frilly ended versions at this point in time but we can see a couple of polar bears (2374) being pretty patriotic!

From this 1917 export catalogue cover peers out what must be one of the jolliest Santas of all. He holds a 'British' cracker in one hand and flags of different nations in the other. This basic cover design was produced in several different colour and design variations between 1917 and the early 1930s.

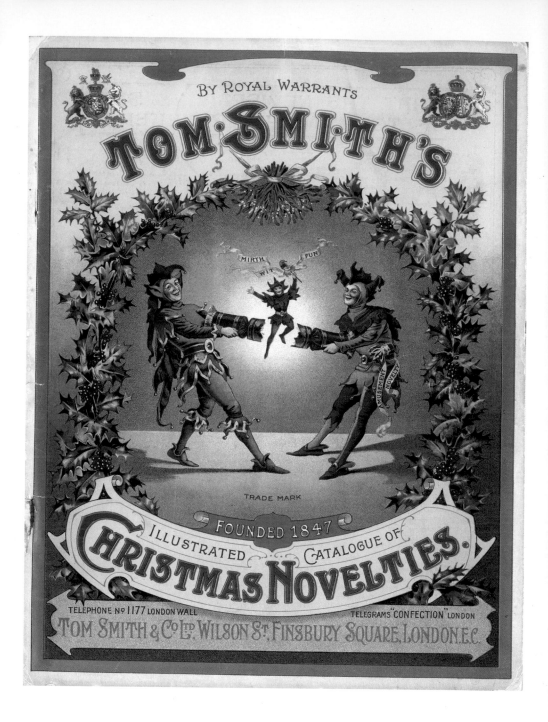

Here in this 1910–11 catalogue cover the company makes play on its Royal Warrants along with holly, mistletoe and jesters.

PLATE O.

TOM SMITH'S
9d. BOX JEWEL CRACKERS.   No. 635

Per Dozen Boxes, 6/9

TOM SMITH'S
COSTUME CRACKERS.   No. 640

Per Dozen Boxes, 8/6

TOM SMITH'S
1/- BOX XMAS JEWELS.   No. 643

Per Dozen Boxes, 9/6

TOM SMITH'S
COSTUME CRACKERS.   No. 577

Per Dozen Boxes, 10/6

TOM SMITH'S
PARLOUR FIREWORKS.   No. 407

Per Dozen Boxes, 7/6

TOM SMITH'S
1/- BOX TOY CRACKERS.   No. 571

Per Dozen Boxes, 8/6

BULLY BOY TOY CRACKERS
No. 646

Per Dozen Boxes, 10/6

TOM SMITH'S
MUSICAL TOY CRACKERS.   No. 576

Per Dozen Boxes, 10/6

LOVE'S GLEANINGS.   No. 637

Per Dozen Boxes, 7/6

TOM SMITH'S 1/- BOX
ASSORTED CRACKERS.   No. 644

Per Dozen Boxes, 9/6

TOM SMITH'S
FAIRY JEWEL CRACKERS.   No. 648

Per Dozen Boxes, 10/6

TOY & PUZZLE CRACKERS.   No. 580

Per Dozen Boxes, 12/6

TOM SMITH & Co., Ltd., Wilson Street, Finsbury, London, E.C.

More amazing designs from the cheaper end of the range in 1910–11. Even at the less expensive end,
the box graphics were great.

PLATE O.

CAPS & JEWELS

209. Per Dozen Boxes, 20/-

TOY CRACKERS

207 Per Doz. Boxes, 16/-

CAPS & TOYS

208. Per Dozen Boxes, 18/-

TOY CRACKERS

217. Per Dozen Boxes, 28/-

FROTH BLOWERS CRACKERS

168 Per Doz. Boxes, 32/-

MASKS, CAPS & BONNETS

162 Per Doz. Boxes, 24/-

TOM SMITH'S LOADS OF FUN

179. Per Dozen Boxes, 50/-

BLINDMAN'S BUFF

175 Per Doz. Boxes, 42/-

MOTORING CRACKERS

165 Per Doz. Boxes, 30/-

TOM SMITH & Co., Ltd., Wilson Street, Finsbury Square, London, E.C.2.

More fine examples of middle-of-the-range crackers. Notice the central design with children blowing bubbles and quaintly referred to as 'Froth Blowers.' These designs come from the end of the 1920s.

PLATE P.

FRIVOLITY CRACKERS

127. Per Dozen Boxes, 48/-

FUN ON A LINER

183. Per Dozen Boxes, 56/-

"JILL" IN THE BOX

233
Per Doz
Boxes,
48/-

FANS AND MONOCLES

180
Per Doz.
Boxes,
52/-

GALA CRACKERS

244. Per Dozen Boxes, 70/-

CUPID'S SEE-SAW

239. Per Dozen Boxes, 56/-

TOM SMITH & Co., Ltd., Wilson Street, Finsbury Square, London, E.C.2.

These 1928–29 offerings were much more from the top end of the company's range – again, super graphics.

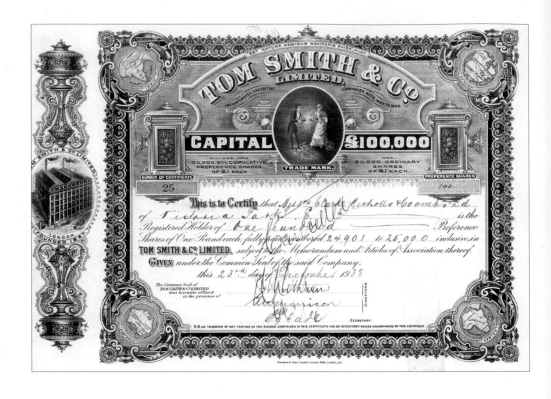

ABOVE *What a pity all share certificates can't look like this beautiful period example from 23 December 1938. Note the handwritten reference to Clarke, Nickolls & Coombs Ltd – 'CLARNICO.'*

OPPOSITE *Pretty children with fancy flower hats. These are beautiful scraps produced by the excellent Mamelok Press – currently the UK's only surviving specialist printer in this field. This example shows how the scraps are initially produced prior to being cut out for use.*

PLATE S.

TOM SMITH'S · ARTISTIC · CRACKERS
FOR
TABLE DECORATION.

4683
52/- per doz. boxes.
12 in a box.

4298
140/- per doz. boxes.
6 in a box.

4682
50/- per doz. boxes.
12 in a box.

4293
70/- per doz. boxes.
6 in a box.

4296
90/- per doz. boxes.
6 in a box.

4291
48/- per doz. boxes.
6 in a box.

4294
78/- per doz. boxes.
6 in a box.

4299
168/- per doz. boxes.
6 in a box.

4280
54/- per doz. boxes.
6 in a box.

4290
44/- per doz. boxes.
6 in a box.

4292
60/- per doz. boxes.
6 in a box.

4686
72/- per doz. boxes.
12 in a box.

4297 100/- per doz. boxes. 6 in a box.

4678
42/- per doz. boxes.
12 in a box.

4295
84/- per doz. boxes.
6 in a box.

TOM SMITH & Co., Ltd., Wilson Street, Finsbury Square, London, E.C.2.

Another page of table decorations from 1930–31. Real fancy creations these and a tribute to the nimble and skilful hands that made them.

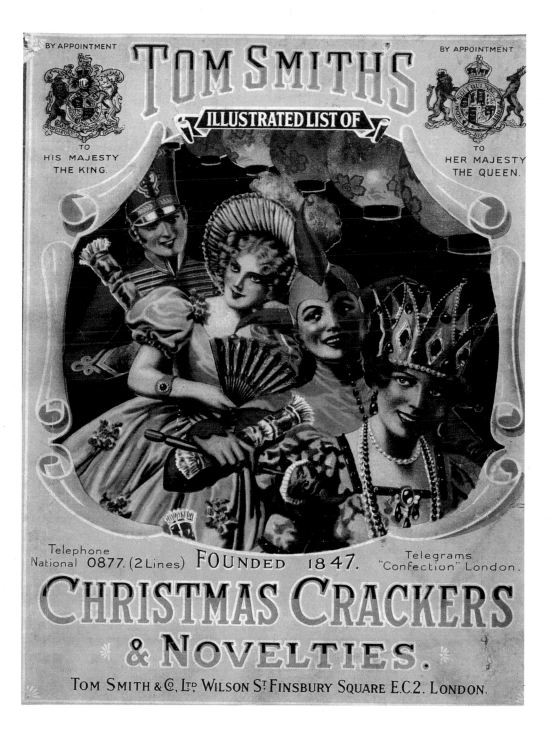

The front cover of the 1934–35 catalogue. Note the figures of the soldier and the girl on the left who bear more than a passing resemblance to those used to promote Mackintosh's Quality Street confectionery from 1936 onwards (see page 123). By kind permission of Amoret Tanner.

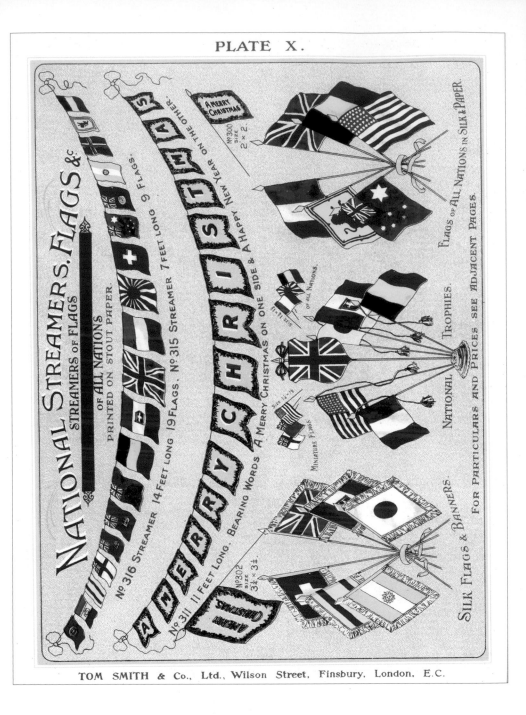

PLATE X.

Flags of assorted nations were also part of the company's range for many years as is depicted by this 1928–29 catalogue page.

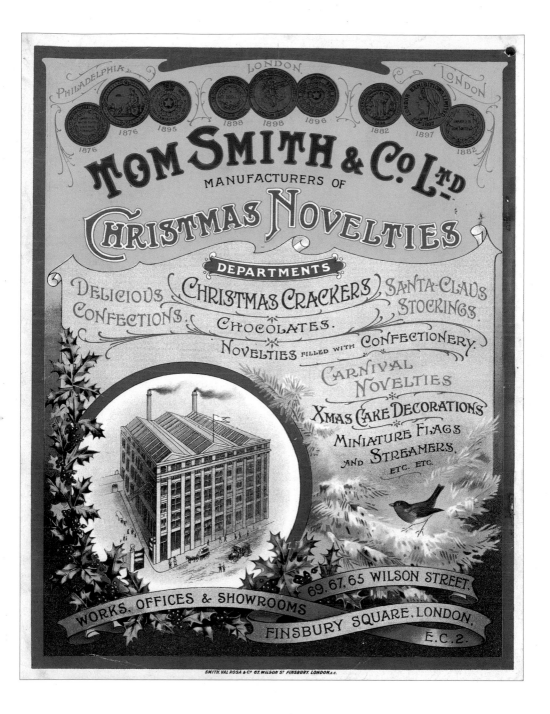

The reverse cover of the 1930–31 catalogue with yet another depiction of the Wilson Street headquarters and with emphasis on a number of medals that the company had been awarded at various exhibitions and trade fairs over the years.

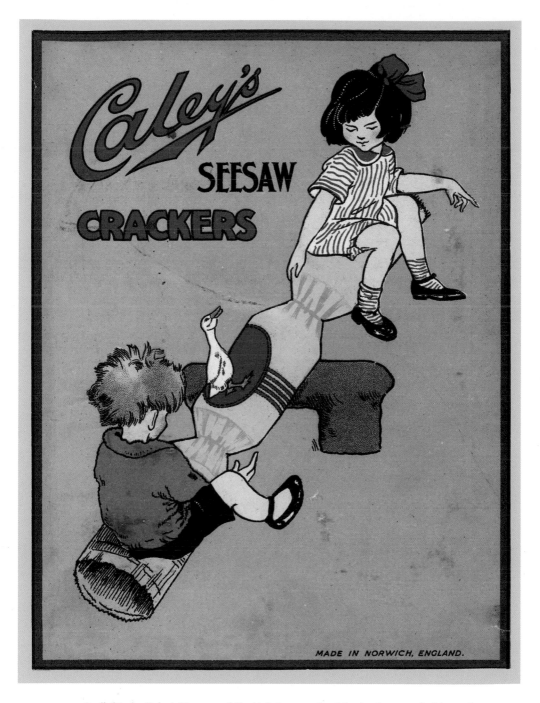

ABOVE *I call this the Caley's 'Seesaw and Duck' design — produced for the cheaper end of the market. The actual date is unknown but probably falls between 1925 and 1935. The children are fun but how on earth did the duck get in on the act?*

OPPOSITE *A children's musical group. Another fine full-sheet example from Mamelok. The subject matter is virtually endless. This example, featuring Victorian children is typical of the period when they were originally produced.*

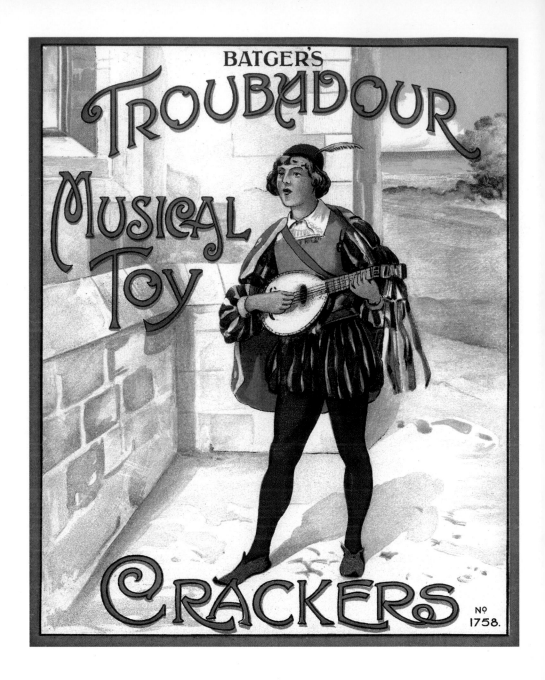

Carol singing was never quite like this as our 'Musical toy' Troubadour strums away outside the medieval window – this design is from the late 1920s.

Beware jesters bearing gifts. The poor old donkey doesn't exactly look full of Christmas cheer as he carries his load in this 'Royal Jester' design, again from Batger's in the late 1920s-early 1930s.

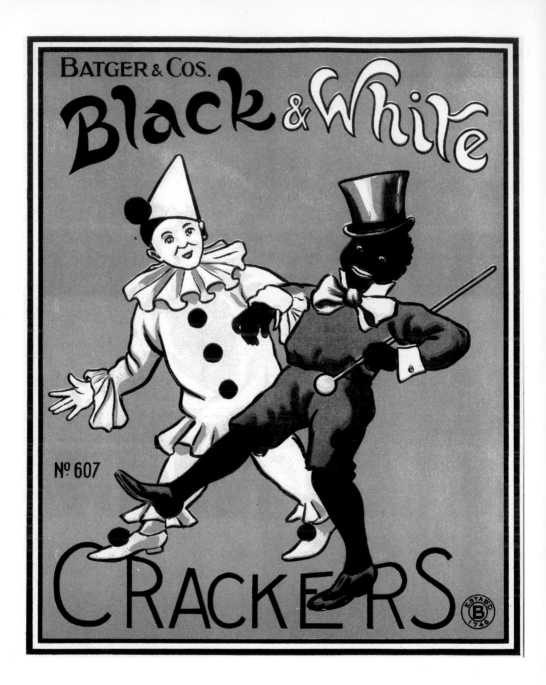

Batger's here again in the late 1920s produced this simple yet mildly racial 'Black & White' design with a clown, hand in hand with his golliwog friend who, in strutting style, appears to have arrived straight off a jar of Robertson's jam! Robertson's used this golliwog figure on numerous items of their packaging over many years.

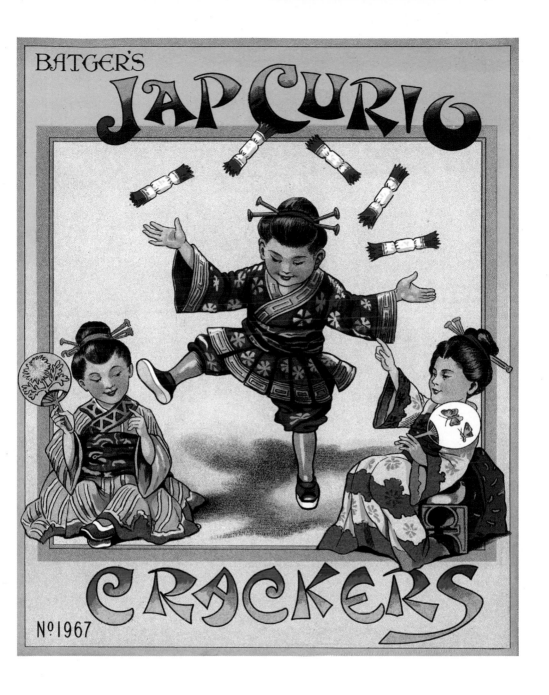

This 'Jap Curio' design, also by Batger's, adds a touch of the mysterious East to the traditional English product.
Another design from around 1925–30.

WE SAY!!!
TOM SMITH'S CRACKERS
TOM SMITH'S
ARE THE BEST.
CAUTION! SEE TOM SMITH'S NAME ON EVERY BOX

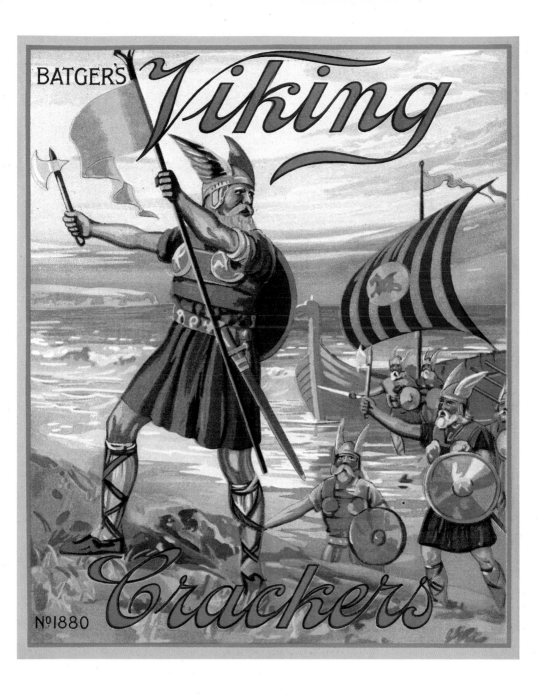

BATGER'S *Viking*

Crackers

Nº1880

ABOVE *The Vikings are coming! Who in the Batger company decided that Viking raiders had anything to do with Christmas crackers remains to be seen, but the end result was this superb example of period graphics from around 1925–30.*

OPPOSITE *This image of our ubiquitous Santa with his young friend were certainly used by Tom Smith's as far back as 1917 and probably earlier. In more modern times, the pair appeared once again on the cover of the company's 1991 catalogue and on actual boxes in 1991–93.*

As detailed on pages 11-12, this fountain in London's Finsbury Square was erected by Walter and Thomas Smith (Tom's sons) to the memory of their mother and Tom's wife Martha – 1826-1898.

SUPERSTITION CRACKERS

THIRTEEN AT DINNER

Of all the superstitions of our race
Thirteen at dinner holds the premier place;
One, so the sages say, must surely die,
So must they all, in time, sense makes reply;
But this advice hug fondly to your breast
— Don't miss your dinner if the thirteenth guest.

Just as with greetings cards today, the mottos were often composed by specialist writers whose task was to come up with witty and up-to-date rhymes and verses that reflected the subject of a particular box of crackers — covering numerous events, fashions and inventions. Similarly, subjects such as suffragette crackers, funny football, motoring, follies, surprise crackers, jewel crackers, signs of the times and Channel Tunnel crackers are all included. One of Smith's trade catalogues of 1891–92 details the names of well-known writers of the time who were persuaded by the company to contribute motto and verse material. Listed are Mr Tom Hood, Mr Charles H. Ross — editor of *Judy*, Mr Ernest Warren — author of *Four Flirts* and *Laughing Eyes*, together with Mr Howard Paul and Mr Edgar Lee.

CHAPTER FIVE

EARLY PRESS COVERAGE

W e all know about the power of the media in today's world but even in those long-gone days of Tom Smith, one of the earliest media references that I have found loosely relating to crackers is an illustration featured on page 424 of the *Illustrated London News* dated 25 December 1847, showing a cracker being pulled by two giant hands, themselves being attached to rather macabre torso-less pairs of legs! It is this particular picture that throws a bit of a complication into the date progression of the development of the cracker, as we shall examine further on. There is nothing to confirm that this page was placed by Tom Smith or indeed that it has anything to do with him but certainly the numerous examples of conundrums that accompany it are very similar to the sort of thing that he would have featured alongside his 'love mottos' in his crackers in the earlier days.

Tom Smith's were no slouches when it came to using the press to their advantage and many of the company's trade catalogues across the decades would copiously quote numerous London newspapers and publications. Sometimes, in a rather tongue-in-cheek way, Smith's referred to these quotations as 'Some of the Latest Criticisms'. Needless to say, all these quotes were fulsome in their praise of their own crackers and the following is a selection from just one trade catalogue of 1891–92:

WHAT THE LONDON PAPERS SAY OF
TOM SMITH'S CRACKERS:

FUN: *'TOM SMITH is the king of Crackers, he stands alone and needs no backers.'*

'Without a word of exaggeration the name of TOM SMITH stands pre-eminent for Crackers.'

FUNNY FOLKS: *'Lest there should be any mistake about the announcement of Messrs TOM SMITH that their Christmas Crackers are the best in the market, we are requested to state that the assertion is not a Cracker.'*

JUDY: *'Go for TOM SMITH, he is the Cracker par excellence.'*

PUBLIC OPINION: *'TOM SMITH'S Crackers are remarkable for freshness, novelty, and originality.'*

PUNCH: *'TOM SMITH'S should have thousands of backers.'*

ST JAMES' GAZETTE: *'TOM SMITH'S Crackers are the Crackers to choose.'*

THE BIRD OF FREEDOM: *'They are the best and most novel design we have seen.'*

THE COURT CIRCULAR: *'TOM SMITH & COMPANY send, as usual, some of the most beautiful Crackers that ever delighted the eyes.'*

'TOM SMITH'S Crackers need no commendation.'

THE DAILY NEWS: *'TOM SMITH'S Crackers are seen everywhere at Christmas time, and this year they are as amusing as ever.'*

'To supply novelties, year after year, is Mr TOM SMITH'S well-sustained boast.'

THE DAILY TELEGRAPH: *'TOM SMITH'S Christmas Crackers, all of which are characterised by ingenuity of invention and felicitous taste.'*

THE ECHO: *'TOM SMITH has elevated the Manufacture of Crackers to a Fine Art.'*

THE ENGLISH CHURCHMAN: *'Mr TOM SMITH'S Crackers are simply wonderful.'*

THE FIGARO: 'No one who has made up his mind to have TOM SMITH'S Crackers will be put off with any others.'

'TOM SMITH'S Crackers once more defy Competition.'

THE GLOBE: 'Ingenuity and taste must have been taxed to their utmost in order to produce such varied designs.'

THE MORNING ADVERTISER: 'TOM SMITH'S ingenuity in providing Novelties for the young is inexhaustible.'

THE NEWS OF THE WORLD: 'TOM SMITH'S Crackers are really works of art.'

THE PALL MALL GAZETTE: 'Mr TOM SMITH is a genius of the first order.'

THE PICTORIAL WORLD: 'TOM SMITH'S Crackers are sure to take the lead.'

THE SPORTING TIMES: 'TOM SMITH is the Champion Cracker Maker.'

THE WORD: 'TOM SMITH'S Crackers have become a perennial institution.'

TRUTH: 'TOM SMITH'S Crackers are by far the best. '

'As to TOM SMITH'S crackers, the more you Crack them the better they are.'

'TOM SMITH more than holds his own.'

Some of the very earliest surviving company catalogues from 1875 and 1877 saw Tom Smith beginning to make use of press quotations and articles in his catalogues, a habit which he and the company practised for many years to come. Certainly the marketing and publicity experts of today, more used to the punchy one-liner, would doubtless question the use of great swathes of copy to sell any product but Tom Smith was nobody's fool and the practice obviously worked for him as his business steadily grew in those earlier years.

One such entry, a tortuous eight-versed poem taken from the Christmas edition of the *Graphic* magazine is entitled 'Grandpa's Lecture On Christmas Crackers'. It reads:

Said Grandpapa to me, as I sat on his knee
The Progress of the Age makes me dumb,
How simple was this toy, when I was a little boy,
And what a smart affair it had become!

The crackers of my youth, were nothing more, in truth,
Than narrow strips of cardboard stuck together,
At the joint, quantum suff, of some explosive stuff,
While a band of coloured paper served as tether.

The fulminating powder seemed to go off all the louder,
When mingled with your partner's exclamation;
Yet this, though very nice, did not for long suffice,
To satisfy the rising generation.

The crackers next grew bigger, and the inner cardboard trigger,
Was concealed within a skin of coloured gum,
Whilst royal kinds of 'sucks,' real confitures de luxe,
Took the place of the primeval sugar plum.

Bigger they waxed and bulkier, prudent papas grew sulkier,
Because these Christmas toys were so expensive
But boys and girls replied, 'Papa! Just look inside,
Was ever anything so comprehensive?

Within the coloured lacquer, which envelopes every cracker,
There are night-caps, mob-caps, aprons, masks and dresses,
And at supper, every night, quite a Babel of delight,
With laughter, shouting, romping and caresses.

That porky quadruped, with a bonnet on his head,
Must be a guest from Skye or from Glencoe,
While every little maiden, her tresses mob-cap laden,
Recalls the days of 'Mademoiselle Angot.'

Now what will be the ending, if crackers keep extending,
And swelling their dimensions every year,
Why, I trust some kindly soul will think up useful doles,

Fill the crackers up with coals,
Joints of meat, or bakers roles, native oysters, turbots, soles –
In short, anything that's seasonable and dear.

What a piece of rambling advertising this is and yet it would appear that busy potential trade customers did actually find the time to stop and read this. But it didn't stop there. As well as items like this, there were often up to six full pages of 'sales pitch' (all in tediously small type!) – but again, it seemed to work as the popularity of the cracker continued apace.

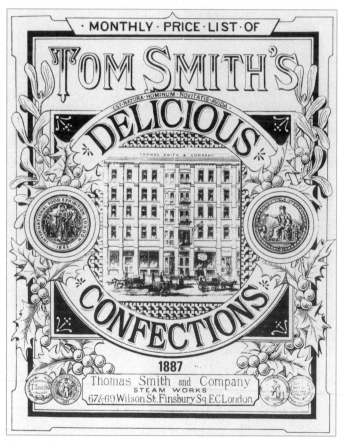

The company's 1887 brochure featured this monthly price list design from 100 years earlier. Note the horse and cart being loaded from the first floor of the factory.

CHAPTER SIX

THREATS FROM HOME & ABROAD

I nitially Tom Smith had only one type of cracker on offer and, as part of his expansion programme, he began to explore the export market.

In all probability, samples must in some way or other have been supplied to potential customers abroad. However, as so often happens, good ideas are often copied (and even more so in Victorian times), and to his dismay a now unknown Eastern manufacturer proceeded to place a large quantity of crackers onto the English market, presumably undercutting the intrepid Mr Smith. What his feelings were at that moment we shall never know, but Tom rose to this challenge in bullish style and, so the story goes, very quickly produced a range of eight other different types of crackers (designs unknown) which, in retaliation, he too placed on to the market to good effect.

While it never appears to have posed any great threat in the UK, there is evidence that around the late 1850s and into the early 1860s the German company of C. Schauer Nachfolger (Berlin, est. 1818) was manufacturing a similar product to the Christmas cracker under the name of 'Silvester's', which were longer and often slimmer than Tom Smith's English versions. These 'crackers' claimed to be safer and were an indoor version of the traditional New Year's fireworks – their name deriving from the German celebration of St Silvester's Eve (New Year's Eve). Even 100 years later, in the late 1950s and early 1960s, Schauer

TOM SMITH'S Christmas Novelties. Season 1906-1907. Show Rooms, 69, Wilson Street, Finsbury, E.C. 3

. Season .
1906-1907

TOM
SMITH'S
Illustrated Christmas
Price . .
List . . . Novelties

LEFT *A catalogue advertisement from 1906–07 still portraying an almost Victorian feel.*

OPPOSITE *From humble beginnings to greater things. The lower picture features Tom Smith's original Goswell Road factory and above, the company's grander premises at Finsbury Square.*

Nachfolger were still producing *Knallbonbons* ('banging sweet' in German) within their range of more than 150 continental-style crackers and decorations.

Although it is uncertain when crackers were first produced in Germany, Dr Christa Pieske's researches tell us that there were quite a few German specialist cracker makers listed over the years. In 1876 there were seven manufacturers in Berlin, most of whom carried on until at least 1914. Also listed in Berlin in 1892 there were eleven manufacturers together with a further three in other parts of Germany. The start of the First World War saw fourteen listed in Berlin and four in other parts. Between the years 1927 and 1935, she mentions a number of makers by name, such as Hoppenworth-E. Petersen; C. Schauer Nachfolger; C. Hering & Co.; Max May; Pohl & Weber and C.F. Leuenberg. In the provinces, Gelbeke & Benedictus in Dresden; Apien-Bennwitz in Leipzig; H. Weissing in Grimma; J. Goetze in Neuruppin and Fr. Schwarze in Greiz. In 1936, only one company is mentioned: Patent-Kartonagenfabrik of Berlin. This company's crackers were produced with lace paper and contained carnival and joke items. Dr Pieske suggests that these crackers were used more exclusively for the carnivals, which took place over the Easter period, and later occasionally at children's parties.

There is one very interesting picture featured in *Das ABC des Luxuspapiers* which shows that outworkers in the cracker trade were not a peculiarly English phenomenon. In a rare image from 1910, we see the kitchen of a house in Berlin (Manteuffstr. 64) in which a mother and two children are busy making *Knallbonbons* at a small table.

A pot of glue is visible. They are assisted by a third girl, probably aged about sixteen who is said to have either TB or pneumonia. The room is in a complete state of disarray, with a bed in one corner, possibly for use by the sick girl. Elsewhere, completed crackers in a large box, various other boxes and a large tin bath litter the floor. On what passes for a kitchen unit, there is a loaf of bread and a lamp among the general clutter. Poor working conditions such as these were typical of the period to the extent that any present-day fire officer wouldn't think twice about classing them as a grade-one fire risk!

Having overcome the immediate threat from the Eastern manufacturer and with no hard evidence having come to light of German

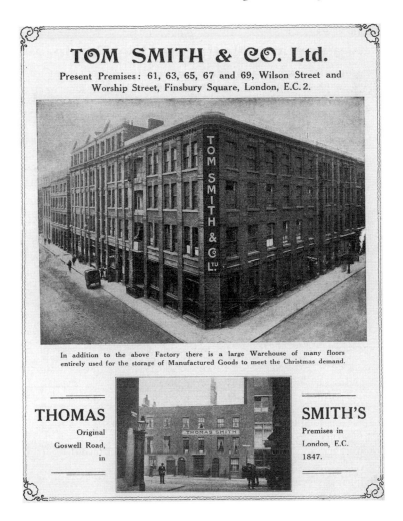

TOM SMITH & CO. Ltd.

Present Premises: 61, 63, 65, 67 and 69, Wilson Street and Worship Street, Finsbury Square, London, E.C. 2.

In addition to the above Factory there is a large Warehouse of many floors entirely used for the storage of Manufactured Goods to meet the Christmas demand.

THOMAS   **SMITH'S**

Original   Premises in
Goswell Road,   London, E.C.
in   1847.

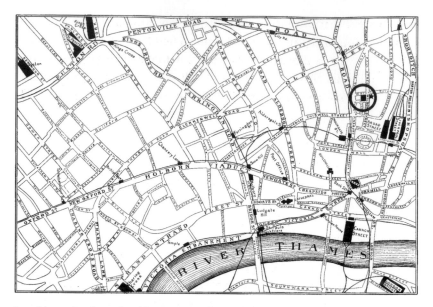

Issued in 1926 and reproduced in numerous other catalogues, this map shows exactly the location of Tom Smith's factory in Wilson Street, London, prior to the move to Norwich in 1953.

manufacturers attempting to sell their wares in the UK, Tom Smith (trading as Thomas Smith in those days) went from strength to strength and his booming business rapidly outgrew the very small Goswell Road factory, pictured in the company's much later 1928–29 trade catalogue, necessitating an eventual move to significantly larger five-storey premises between Wilson Street (which still exists today) and Worship Street, Finsbury Square, also in London. Catalogue covers of the time refer to the factory as The Steamworks and we can only speculate that this was taken from the fact that equipment within the factory – a representation of which is featured on the reverse cover of several of his trade catalogues (and the reverse cover of this book) – was indeed powered by steam. Those same catalogues also show that for those customers who wanted to place an order or make an enquiry, Tom Smith's at this time could be reached on the rather quaint early telephone number of Clerkenwell 1177.

On the home front, Tom Smith had his competitors, many of whom preferred to offer their products anonymously with neither the maker's nor product's name appearing on the box. Probably by intention, many of these covert cracker makers were riding on Tom Smith's reputation to the extent that during the 1890s and even through to the 1930s the company (originally incorporated under The Companies Acts of 1862–1900) issued stern threats, via its trade catalogue, of legal proceedings under the Trades Mark Act to all those who sought to compete unfairly. Other warnings were often in the form of earnest notices to the trade with such statements as:

> *It is deemed important to caution the Trade against the incalculable injury that is being done by small manufacturers in putting forth Monster Boxes of Gaudy and Vulgar Crackers lacking appreciable contents; the effects upon the purchaser being keen disappointment, and upon the retailer an undeserved odium and the loss of custom. The Trade, therefore, for their own reputation, are advised against purchasing Christmas Crackers other than those bearing Tom Smith's Name.*

Strong words but this competition must have been significantly nibbling away at Smith's share of the cracker market to warrant this particular 'warning'. It was also not uncommon to see the statement 'See Tom Smith's Name On Every Box'.

At this point, I would like to discuss briefly the subject of the 'mysterious Italian'. There has been some speculation that a Mr Hovell had

 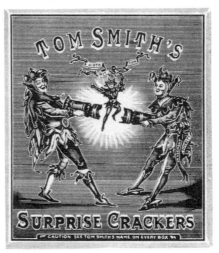

LEFT *This winged cherub in 'Jack-in-the-box' pose pops up to warn potential customers once again – 'Caution!! Ask for and see you get Tom Smith's'.*

RIGHT *A 1910–11 advertisement featuring jesters – offering 'Mirth, Fun and Wit!' Note the ubiquitous caution of 'SEE TOM SMITH'S NAME ON EVERY BOX.'*

actually invented the cracker. Prior to the takeover of Tom Smith's in 1985, the Hovell's company were claiming that their founder, also a confectioner, was producing crackers in 1854 but you will remember that on page 15 we gave Tom Smith the benefit of the doubt. However, there are some other points to consider. The Christa Pieska material refers to material by a journalist named Henry Mayhew who, in 1850, wrote an article for the *Morning Chronicle* concerning the smaller cracker manufacturers of the time. In it, Mayhew described the workshop of an Italian cracker manufacturer in London and how he would deliver crackers to the big houses of the wealthy – at the servants' entrance, of course! Mayhew also suggested that the Italian was supposed to have the secret of cracker manufacture and was purported to have made around 750,000 in one year, which at twelve to a box would have been over 60,000 boxes. Quantities like that would have made him a serious competitor to Tom Smith or, at the very least, something of an irritant.

But let us look at the matter a little more closely. With Smith having founded his business in 1847 and presumably, over the next few years, offering the public his bonbon-based non-exploding version ('Christmas Bonbonnes – complete with surprise'), what was happening in the intervening years until 1860, when he announced his 'Bangs of Expectation'? Is it conceivable that if the Italian had indeed actualised the idea by 1850, Smith would have taken another decade or so to work out the 'exploding' concept for himself? I think not. Of course, it could have been that Mayhew himself was purely referring to the non-exploding version.

On the other hand, could it be that Tom Smith had the concept pretty much tied up long before he supposedly announced it in 1860? Were the 'Bangs of Expectation' just another marketing ploy – a fresh promotional description for the product that had existed for a number of years anyway? Certainly the 1847 *Illustrated London News* illustration seems to show an exploding cracker.

It is also pertinent to consider the recollections of Eric Varnon, a senior member of the Tom Smith company for many years, who recalled the story concerning the father of one of the company's employees in London in 1936. This man's father supposedly helped Tom Smith in the successful development of the 'snap' effect over a two-year period in the 1850s. Although this story sadly cannot be confirmed by the present generation of the Varnon family, if this experimentation indeed took place during the latter part of the decade, then the introduction of the 'Bangs of Expectation' was chronologically correct.

And so finally, who gets the credit? Could it be that the mystery Italian was indeed the true inventor of the cracker as we know it? As with many historical events that are not particularly well documented, these questions can of course only remain a matter for our speculation and will almost certainly never be satisfactorily answered. However, if you are of Italian decent and have a grandfather several times removed, who made and sold crackers in London in 1850, please get in touch and maybe we can solve the riddle once and for all!

Moving on to the middle of the twentieth century, stiff competition was still around and one of those competitors was College Crackers, which had sprung up during the 1950s in Royal College Street, London, as a response to the disappearance of many companies as a direct result of the war. Like most other major players in the industry, College, in the 1980s, produced its own glossy annual catalogue but its relative youth as a company, however, meant that it had no real long-term past tradition and doesn't seem to have retained anything much by way of significant archive material.

Another sizeable competitor was Mead & Field, who in 1929 were operating from the Cracker Works in Holborn. Catalogues from that year until 1970 show Mead & Field, like others, to have been producing fairly ordinary material, with perhaps the exceptions of illuminated cracker novelties and, listed in 1957, rather strange items called Carnival Follies – which were something akin to the old jester's sticks and were possibly intended to be waved at parties or fêtes. The year 1938 had also seen the availability of something called a Jollibomb – an exploding tube filled with novelties. Today, items like this would almost certainly fall into the category of Indoor Fireworks, which they offered in cracker format also.

Among other names that have come and gone in the past are Mansells and miniature cracker specialist Batger & Co. (advertising themselves as 'Creators of Joy' and astonishingly originally established as a company in 1748 – long before the invention of crackers). Batgers were certainly producing crackers from around 1900 onwards and possibly earlier, offering some superb box designs during the first twenty or thirty years of the twentieth century, the quality of which is reflected in such gems as Jolly Old Monks, Funniosity, Animal Luggage and the colour-ful Speedboat crackers which they produced for the illustrious Harrods store in London. Two other manufacturers were Harlequin Crackers from the 1930s period and Rainbow Crackers, both of whom were subsequently acquired by College. College in its turn fell upon hard times in the mid-1990s and, as a result of its receivership, was purchased by Napier Industries.

Companies such as Barratts, Sharps, Fanfare, the Manler Manufacturing Company of Chesterfield, Chatsworth and Bennett Bros have all come to light but the likelihood is that several, if not all of these, were cracker stockists rather than manufacturers. Another was Brocks Crackers who were certainly producing crackers in the 1930s, with a design featur-ing a female harlequin although whether this particular company was anything to do with the famous firework company, I have been unable to confirm. Smith's 1888–89 catalogue also makes note of the fact that, for reasons now unknown, they were offering Baldwin's crackers – a company name I have never heard of before.

In North America, at least up until the late 1960s, the Canadian firm of Somerville Industries Ltd of Toronto under the brand name of 'Strathmore' were producing fairly ordinary crackers and an undated catalogue in the Victoria & Albert museum archive shows the Scandinavian firm of G. Ahrenkiel (established in 1877) producing crackers of a continental style in Denmark. Another name that has also twice come to light during the preparation of this book – from both Canadian and UK sellers on eBay who were both offering undated boxes of old crackers – was a company named Sparagnapanes of whom I have no other information. And finally, the similarly unfamiliar UK names of Plaistow & Co. Ltd of Kings Cross in London which also appeared recently on the internet with a design called 'Jolly Good Fellows' from around 1910, Liptons Paper Mills Ltd and the unusually named Kaputine Ltd of Oldham, Lancashire.

Mason & Church, who are listed as having been operating in Croydon in 1935, were taken over by Smith's in 1967 and while little of that compa-ny's early history can be found, it is clear from catalogues of 1973 to 1982 that Smith's were still using the Mason & Church brand name at that time and offering around a dozen varieties of crackers seemingly aimed at the bottom end of the market. The scraps being used on these particular crackers were accordingly pretty cheap affairs, as were the contents.

CHAPTER SEVEN

UNCLE SAM'S FAIR LAND

Let's talk about crackers in the USA. Details are fairly thin on the ground and only a relatively small amount of information has come to light about the product in that particular country – especially pre-1900. It seemed sensible therefore to group together both the nineteenth and twentieth-century material in this section.

At this point I must especially give mention to the knowledgeable John Grossman in the USA who, from his own excellent collection of Christmas and related material built up over many years, has helped me with several pieces of information concerning the American 'scene'. He confirms that crackers were apparently a fairly minor part of American Christmas celebrations and were not widespread. Within his collection, he has uncovered an 1880s chromolithographed trade stock card based on a photograph of four children around a Christmas tree showing several crackers as part of the tree decorations. The card is also imprinted with the merchant's name and comes from Allenstown, Pennsylvania.

On the Eastern seaboard, a catalogue from J. Jay Gould, a Boston merchant who specialised in chromos, scrap pictures and other novelties, dated 1885, offers

Costumes and Mottos for Children Made in Germany. One dozen pack-
ages in a box. Each contains a nicely made cap, night-cap, hood, apron,
cape, and collar etc etc, made wholly of paper, usually pure white paper;

each package, besides containing one of the above articles contains a motto and snapper, designed especially for children's parties, making more fun than anything else in the world, for instance, give one package to each of a fun-loving party of boys and girls, each immediately open their package, after first reading their motto and snapping their snapper to see what their prize is, then the fun commences, some boy will find a night-cap, some girl a smoking-cap, others will have large white capes, aprons etc, of every comical shape with which they will quickly attire themselves and wear the whole evening, creating a great deal of laughter and many harmless jokes at the expense of those that are so unlucky as to draw a night-cap, as they will be the 'old maid' for the evening, and will have to pay all forfeits that the others may make. Put up in nice little rolls, about six inches long, by one inch in diameter, with outer case of coloured gelatine paper. Each end of package nicely fringed. Sample, by mail, 15 cents. One dozen packages $1.20. Very attractive ornament for Christmas tree.'

Note how Mr Gould refers to each cracker as a package and I just love his exaggerated claim of 'making more fun than anything else in the world'. Glowing but unprovable praise indeed from a man in dire need of a course in punctuation. If you have the time to stop and count; the preceding sentence has over 170 words and not a single full stop! All great fun.

In his collection John has full-page political Christmas cartoons from the *Judge* and *Puck* publications dated 1894 showing crackers as part of the illustrations. He also has two boxes of 'U-Neak Snapping Mottos, The Favorite of All Containing Jewellery, Musical Instruments, Games, Caps and Snappers. Each Motto has Double Contents (A Favor and a Hat). Made By S.D. & N. Co., N.Y. City'. A small label on the bottom of each box identifies them as from the toy department of 'The White House, San Francisco, Cal.' – which was a very famous department store at the time. Here the crackers were referred to as snappers and inside the boxes are, complete with Santa, die-cut scrap decorations. These particular boxes appear to be dated 1915.

In his 1985 book *December 25* Phillip Snyder refers to a postcard published by Curt Teich of Chicago and postmarked 'Arkansas' in the Deep South and dated 1907. It features a Punch-like figure and a pine cone character pulling on a large cracker. The handwritten message on the reverse makes mention of all the noise from the celebration fireworks and it is reasonable to assume that crackers would certainly have been part of those activities.

Snyder also notes

An article in The Atlantic Monthly in 1884 described a party where the tree had been hidden behind a sheet. Before they could see the wonders of the tree, the children were treated to a magic lantern show projected onto the sheet. Then a chorus of "Ah's" was heard as the sheet was drawn aside, revealing a big tree aglow with candles and topped with an angel. The family gardener stood by with a bucket of water, just in case. The Christmas tree was loaded with baubles and little presents that were distributed all round. Then the room "resounded with joyful voices inter-mingled with exclamations of surprised triumph; paper cups, and aprons, and bonnets, and mottos in the most execrable verse that ever the wit of man devised. There were a due quota of penny whistles, trumpets and accordions. The oranges and bonbons from the tree were followed by slices of cake from the table".'

Presumably crackers must have played their part in celebrations such as these.

He further compares 'modern' popping, confetti-filled versions of crackers (favors) – used mainly for birthdays, with the Victorian scene in which crackers held more sway, with expectant children awaiting the 'bang' and the subsequent scrambling for the surprises which flew out. Among a number of novelties he mentions were pipes and false moustaches together with a bottle of 'gin' sporting a label announcing 'One Million Overproof' – hardly sound guidance to the children of the day for sobriety in adulthood!

Among Phillip Snyder's interesting work, however, I must take issue with his statement that 'The Christmas cracker originated in France.' While I would fully agree that *bonbons* very probably originated in France, because that is where Tom Smith is supposed to have seen them originally, I feel it is only fair to say that the true cracker as we know it today only came into being as a result of Mr Smith's experiments in the UK when he developed the bonbon by adding the 'snap' effect, which the French product never had.

Another point worth remembering is that around the time that Tom Smith was promoting his 'Bangs of Expectation' in the UK in the early

1860s, our American cousins between 1861 and 1865 were themselves experiencing some very serious internal disagreements with the Civil War. It seems fairly reasonable therefore to assume that the importation of crackers at that point in time was pretty low on their list of priorities! As such, it must have been some years until the cracker established some sort of presence across the 'pond.'

The hard fact of the matter is that in America, a country currently with a population approaching 300 million, the English Christmas cracker has never truly caught on to the same degree that it has in the UK and a true national cracker 'tradition' has never really been established. Maybe it never will be. Certainly in America, as discussed, they were treated as much more of a fun item, whereas in England they were taken rather more seriously. Yes, crackers do sell in substantial numbers in the USA today and there are many importers and retailers but for the size of the country and with such an ethnically diverse population, many without a 'cracker' background and tradition, sales pro rata are still relatively modest. In those earlier years of the twentieth century, the Americans in fact didn't tend to call crackers 'crackers' at all and often used the terms: mottos, snappers, snapping bonbons, snapping mottos or motto favors. One company, Dennison Co., seemingly not wanting any nasty surprises and apparently showing a certain unease with the 'snap' effect of the crackers, offered them for sale as serviette rings or napkins filled with hats or masks. On a lighter note, crackers did seem to have an attraction for those dance enthusiasts holding 'flapper' parties, the same being the case in the UK.

In the later years of the nineteenth century and the earlier years of the twentieth century, most if not all crackers sold in the USA were imported. Many retail and wholesale catalogues of companies of the period, now long gone, offered pages and pages of crackers for sale but sadly most were unillustrated. What fairly sparse information there is concerning the retail sector is covered by Dr Christa Pieske who notes that, in 1903, the company Wannamaker-Laden strangely listed the crackers they had on offer amongst their range of confectionery.

OPPOSITE *Proof if proof were needed of the spread of Tom Smith's name across the world. With 'Father Tom Smith' astride a giant cracker, this advertisement somehow turned up in Maine, USA, and looks to be based on company advertising material from around the late 1920s. Note how the company is still pushing the inferiority of its competitor's products.*

Father Tom Smith Arrives!

Here he comes again! loaded up with a big bag of crackers —bright-hued ones—the sight of them thrills you with the Christmas Spirit. Good old Father Tom Smith! He only comes once a year but what good cheer he always brings!

TOM SMITH'S
CHRISTMAS CRACKERS

At prices from 8 cents up to $2.50 per dozen, they described them as 'an elegant assortment.'

The year 1910 saw two companies – B. Shackman and F.A.O. Schwartz (a large New York toy shop) – both offering crackers. Shackman, in their party items catalogue listed crackers at prices from 25 cents up to $1 and with Schwartz coming in at 10 cents to $1.25 for crackers containing 'Paper hats, toys, jewellery and musical instruments'. The year 1920 saw The American Supply company offering 'motto savers' containing 'full-size hats made of material.'

As a final note, and from a marketing and sales point of view, it is worth remembering that for any European company exporting a product like the cracker to distant places such as the USA, the manufacturer, due to the basic construction of the product, is faced with the problem of transporting what in reality is a box containing an awful lot of air, which will obviously reflect the final retail price and thus the margin to be made.

Chapter Eight

A NEW AGE

THE NEXT GENERATION

Upon his death Tom Smith was survived by his three sons (and two daughters) – Henry, Walter and Tom junior who, after their father's death, between them took over the running of the business. It was Walter Smith (at one time becoming a Finsbury councillor) who in particular introduced a more topical tone to many of the mottos, and it is said that was also responsible for the introduction of the tissue paper hats that we know so well today. Walter seems, on the face of it, to have been the more prominent of the three brothers and certainly took some interest in local public affairs. At the turn of the century, he was quoted as being in favour of the London County Council employing local labour on trade union conditions although whether he practised these laudable ideals in this own factory is unknown.

INTO THE TWENTIETH CENTURY

With the twentieth century having arrived and with Queen Victoria having passed from the scene her son, Edward VII, took the throne. Tom Smith's at this time (albeit servicing a smaller national population than today) was, around 1900, producing the considerable total of around 13 million crackers per year – the majority of which were destined for the UK market although exports played their part. Interestingly, Pieske

Walter Smith – Tom's third son, pictured in the Lady
*magazine of 1911 as part of the article entitled 'The Castle
of the Cracker King'.*

comes up with Tom Smith's annual production figures for the year 1909
and gives a total of 11 million, of which between 8 and 9 million were
for the domestic market. If this figure is to be accepted, it would indicate an unexplained dip in the market at a time when crackers were
arguably at their most popular, although it could merely have reflected
Smith's competitors gaining more market share.

Having said that, from this distance in time it is virtually impossible
to verify any of Smith's annual cracker production figures, but if Christa
Pieska's figure of 11,000,000 for 1909 is to be accepted, then it is interesting that only two years later, in 1911, E.M. Tait's figure in The Castle
of the Cracker King (page 124) gives an annual total of 25,000,000!
Progress indeed!

Always a labour-intensive industry (a bit of a sweatshop some might
say) girls, often on piece work, inserted the appropriate knick-knack and
would complete the process of tying, gluing and packing (see Appendix
Four: 'The Castle of the Cracker King') – all for pretty low wages at that
time. One piece of reference for the year 1900 suggests that the girls
were making around two dozen crackers in fifteen minutes.

In around 1990 I remember interviewing a then very elderly Mrs
Matilda Kitson who had joined Tom Smith's in London in 1921, and
had worked her way up to the position of Cracker Room supervisor
by 1936. One of the highlights of her career was in 1967 when she was
specially sent to the famous Gimbles department store in Pittsburgh,
USA, in the United States to demonstrate the great and peculiarly
British art of cracker making during its Great Britain week there.

There is more from and about Matilda (now sadly demonstrating her talents in the great Christmas cracker factory in the sky) in Chapter Thirteen: Personal Recollections.

All these crackers, of course, needed to be filled with novelties and Tom Smith's sourced various small items from all four corners of the globe, including cheap jewellery, glassware and the like from Bohemia, fans and paper products from China, jade and ivory artefacts from India and little hand-made wooden toys from Norway. There were also novelties from such places as America, Africa and Turkey, as well as from the UK, and finally on a more sophisticated note, fine perfumes from France and musical toys from both France and Germany.

One of the less than complimentary labels attributed to Christmas crackers over the years concerns the cracker contents. How often is the comment heard that the contents of Christmas crackers are 'totally worthless', or 'cheap plastic rubbish'? To be fair to all concerned, especially the manufacturers, it stands to reason that if you are only paying two or three pounds for a box of twelve crackers, you are not going to get the Crown Jewels! On the other hand, it does not take a genius to deduct that the more you are prepared to pay, the better the contents!

CRACKERS AS GIFTS

Reference to old sales catalogues reveal the fact that in Victorian times and reaching into the early part of the twentieth century boxes of crackers, or even individual crackers, were given much more as gifts. This, together with the ability to target topical events, was almost certainly one of the reasons for the extent of Tom Smith's cracker range and its diversity of subject.

There is one very poignant but true story from 1927 when one love-struck young gentleman, at least I assume he was young, wrote to the company enclosing a gold and diamond engagement ring for his intended, together with a ten-shilling note (50p in today's money) and a letter asking that a special cracker be prepared and the ring be inserted as an offering for his lady. Sadly, our love-struck gentleman – his thoughts obviously distracted by amorous intentions elsewhere – forgot to enclose his address and, for whatever reason, he never contacted the company again. I once held this ring and letter and it posed the question did they ever marry? Was he rejected? We shall

One of the bigger efforts! A 1981 giant 12ft cracker produced at Tom Smith's Salhouse Road factory in Norwich and carried by eleven smiling staff.

never know but the ring, the letter and ten-shilling note still remain safely guarded somewhere in the archives to this day.

SPECIAL REQUESTS

During its existence the Tom Smith company has fulfilled many requests for special crackers from large to small, plain to fancy. The 1920s in turn produced an order for the company to produce what at the time was the largest cracker ever made. The length was some eighteen feet and such was the girth that when 'pulled' at a banquet in London, a number of waitresses were able to walk out from inside and distribute gifts. Larger still, although not made by Tom Smith's, was a massive version 63.1 metres long and with a diameter of 4 metres. Claimed as the largest cracker in the world, this whopper was made by the children of Ley Hill in Buckinghamshire and was 'pulled' in December 2001. Probably not the ideal size for granny's dining room! Sadly, the days of very special productions are now few and far between. Expense coupled with modern bulk-production methods unfortunately mean that special one-off items are rare. Today, in the early twenty-first century, some cracker companies still do make 'giant' crackers but 'giant' in today's terms usually means something of merely around 1 metre long.

CHAPTER NINE

WARTIME HARDSHIPS

SHORTAGES IN THE FIRST WORLD WAR

The First World War was no respecter of people or commerce and, whether by the appropriation of industrial plant, manpower or materials, called upon many things which are so often taken for granted. Because of these shortages, Tom Smith's was forced to include various notices 'to the Trade' within the catalogues of the time to justify increased prices due to shortages of various raw materials.

Few items were easily obtainable any more and this was illustrated by notices in the company's product catalogue in January 1917, which also included a leaflet promoting crackers and stockings based on the fact that there had been a shortage of Continental supplies of children's toys, and tinplate toys and novelties together with the jewellery which came from Bohemia.

It is also noticeable at this time that much of Tom Smith's advertising material became very patriotic, with boxes of crackers and brochures featuring designs such as Union Jacks, smiling soldiers, red-cross nurses, bombs of peace, the United Kingdom, united forces, British heroes, big guns, jolly Jack tars, victory crackers and many other militaristic designs; all no doubt created to promote national pride and patriotism in a time of trouble.

Having said all this and despite the shortages, life at home, with the hostilities seemingly so far away, must, to a degree, have carried on

HIGHEST AWARD, FRANCO-BRITISH EXHIBITION, 1908.

MOTOR TRANSPORT WAGGON. No. 3194.

A cardboard model Motor Transport Waggon of the Army Service Corps, 12¼ ins. × 5¾ ins., packed full with 12 Crackers in Red, White, Blue and Khaki, containing Hats, Caps, Toy Pistols, Guns, Cannon, Soldiers, and War Shooting Pictures.

Per dozen Waggons **15/-**

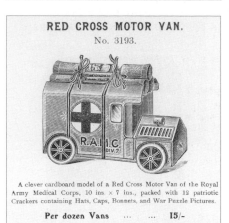

RED CROSS MOTOR VAN.
No. 3193.

A clever cardboard model of a Red Cross Motor Van of the Royal Army Medical Corps, 10 ins. × 7 ins., packed with 12 patriotic Crackers containing Hats, Caps, Bonnets, and War Puzzle Pictures.

Per dozen Vans **15/-**

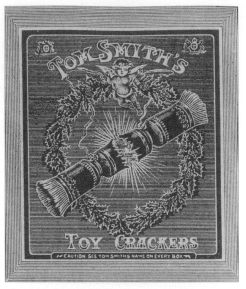

KHAKI HAT. No. 3191.

Packed into a real Khaki Hat of correct shape are 12 Red, White and Blue Crackers containing Hats, Toy Guns, Pistols, Cannon, etc.

Per dozen Hats **18/-**

TOM SMITH'S ART JEWEL CRACKERS.
No. 947.

Containing pretty and artistic articles of imitation Jewellery, such as Necklets, Bracelets, Charms, Brooches, Pins, Pendants, etc., together with Fortune-telling Mottoes. The Crackers are designed in Crimson Gelatines with Gold Ends, and are decorated with medallion pictures of Lovely Women.

Per dozen boxes **18/-**

TOP *A smiling young soldier grapples with an armful of flags of all nations in this advertisement from a 1917 wartime export catalogue.*

MIDDLE AND BOTTOM *A pair of novelty cracker boxes in the form of cardboard vehicles from around 1917. Both product descriptions and contents indicate very obvious war association.*

TOP *Blissfully unaware, yet another smiling cherub seems too close for comfort as this 1917 wartime export catalogue advert depicts a satisfyingly large 'crack'. Notice the fringed cracker ends — a greatly used feature on crackers from its early days and for many years to come.*

BOTTOM *More First World War associations with this very unusual cracker-filled novelty container under the title of 'Khaki Hat' from 1917.*

WAR CONDITIONS.

We are anxious to express full appreciation to our numerous friends and customers for their indulgence during the very trying time we have experienced all through the recent Christmas Season.

DEPLETION OF STAFF.

SHORTAGE OF RAW MATERIAL.

TRAFFIC DISLOCATION.

We realise that notwithstanding the above, inconvenience may have been caused to some of our friends and to these we beg to express our regrets.

Through the continued difficulties we are sorry to have to intimate that orders can only be accepted subject to our being able to supply.

It is urgently requested that orders be placed as early as possible, and that a wide margin be given for shipment by stating the earliest and latest date for goods to arrive.

Christmas Crackers, Santa Claus Stockings, Wreaths, Cake Ornaments, Patriotic Flags, &c.

Most of the quotations in this Catalogue having been arranged before the enormous rise in labour and material (amounting to over 50 %) T. S. & Co., Ltd., are sacrificing a large percentage of their profit, and beg to intimate to their customers that $33\frac{1}{3}$ % will be added to the invoices of all goods ordered from this List on pages 3 to 48 and pages 61 and 65.

Should any line be out of stock, the nearest in contents and price will be substituted.

The above increase of $33\frac{1}{3}$ % and the remaining pages, viz., 49 to 60 are subject to market fluctuations.

January, 1917.   **TOM SMITH & CO. LTD.**

Times were getting harder! Wartime difficulties with staff, materials and transport prompted this early 1917 notification (with regret!) of price increases by one third.

unchanged in many ways. Few folks back home could have been totally unaware of the extent of carnage going on in the war and yet it seems strange that a fair number of Smith's designs featured military subjects with a slightly humorous slant. However, it goes without saying that the poor devils being blasted into oblivion in the trenches of northern France would have given their eye teeth (and probably did!) to have been at home pulling a few crackers with their loved ones!

'DON'T PANIC, CAPTAIN MAINWARING'

The hostilities of the Second World War had meant that the usual cracker-making materials were diverted elsewhere and no crackers were produced during this period. Wars, however, often throw up strange stories and there is one rather odd, even amusing, historical footnote regarding the use of cracker snaps during the Second World War. Shortages of many things during the early period of hostilities (and in this case I refer to bullets or at least blanks!) meant that the production of cracker snaps by the Reliance Snap company was only permitted by the Ministry of Defence strictly for military purposes. In what from this distance in time seems to be an almost ludicrous exercise, Tom Smith's, using 'regulation' knots, had been required to fold and tie together bundles of between three and six snaps. These bundles, which were very similar in look to the old 'Jumping Jack' fireworks, were then used in troop training, with the traditional story telling that when a string was pulled on the bundle of snaps (which had previously been fixed to the soldier's belt), the resulting effect supposedly mimicked real gunfire.

However, the more expert opinion of David Penn – Keeper of Exhibits and Firearms at the Imperial War Museum – suggests that it was more probable that the bundle of snaps was likely to have been attached to wooden dummy firearms or machine guns to simulate fire.

Troop training with a difference:
Seemingly in the best traditions of the eccentric madcap British inventor, this concept (of which this example has amazingly survived) is one of the many weird and wonderful inventions that surfaced during the Second World War, and must surely rank as one of the least credible. Having been tied together – as pictured above, these bundles of cracker snaps were, according to expert David Penn, attached to wooden dummy/replica firearms with the resulting effect supposedly representing gunfire when the string was pulled! Photo by kind permission of the trustees of the Imperial War Museum.

Whether you choose to accept the more traditional version which has been around for many years or go for David's more expert opinion, both scenarios can only be described as laughable in today's world of sophisticated weaponry. But either choice would surely have provoked from the blustering Captain Mainwaring of *Dad's Army* fame the world-renowned chastisement of 'You stupid boy, Pike!' Could it be in hindsight that news of these 'advanced' training techniques with their 'regulation' knots and folded cracker snaps had filtered through to the bunker in Berlin and were perhaps one of the deciding factors in persuading a dithering Hitler to delay his invasion of England? The mind boggles!

Another interesting footnote to the history of the cracker in wartime was that, even in 1940, such was the enduring tradition of the product that at least some crackers (possibly home made) are known to have been sent within Red Cross parcels to RAF prisoners of war in such places as the German Stalag Luft camp in the Baltic.

Upon the cessation of wartime hostilities, huge quantities of by-now surplus packs of the folded snaps were released back to members of the cracker trade via the Acme Board company who, when these stocks ran out, established an agency with the Reliance Snap company to supply snaps to the ever-growing number of smaller cracker manufacturers.

Continuing shortages in the wake of the Second World War had, for obvious reasons, caused a reduction in quality from the fine standards set in Victorian and Edwardian times and my own feeling, albeit subjective, is that those previous aesthetic levels have never been reached again. As is the case with many things in our lives, quality and standards seem to decline with the passing of time and prices seem ever to rise!

CHAPTER TEN

MERGERS
AND TAKEOVERS

O ver the years, there have been numerous Christmas cracker manufacturers – many now long forgotten, but none has been more famous or had more influence on the cracker industry since its early beginnings than Tom Smith's during the nineteenth and twentieth centuries. For many, Tom Smith was *the* Christmas cracker and the Christmas cracker *was* Tom Smith, and many of the newspapers and publications of the times attested to this. Its London roots at 65-69 Wilson Street, Finsbury Square, were left well and truly behind in 1953 when it merged with Caley Crackers, based at the 'Fleur De Lys' works in Norwich.

Many of the early Caley box designs featured graphics produced by a young A.J. Munnings – an East Anglian artist (1878–1959) – who at the beginning of his career, worked as a designer for the Norwich printers Page Bros and went on to become so internationally celebrated in later years. Munnings had been apprenticed to Page Bros in 1891–92, with his father paying a £40 premium. He worked his way up among the six artists in the 'Artists Room' – who helped him learn his trade including, of course, all that was involved in the preparation of the chromolithographic process, which was capable of producing such superb printing. The basic hours were quite long – 9 a.m. to 7 p.m. – and his talents meant Munnings was often overloaded with work. One of his designs won him a gold medal in a London poster competition and he produced brilliant design ideas for many different types of products, including lemonade, chocolates, mustard, whisky, pills and, of course, Caley Christmas crackers.

There were times when Munnings had extra special successes and one in particular was a poster for Caley crackers featuring 'Elizabethan 'prentice boys in red running up a street in the snow.' It was just after 1918 and this piece of his work finished up on many hoardings all over London. He recalled, 'How happy I was when I had a new batch of cracker boxes to do', and his enthusiasm was well reflected in one truly beautiful design that was featured on a poster and depicted goblins, pixies and a spider with a web. Other fine examples of work by the great man that still survive today are the wonderful and well-known 'Queen of Hearts,' 'Friar of Orders Grey,' 'Jack and the Giant-Killer,' 'Young and Old,' and Caley's 'Christmas Pudding' crackers featuring, as the name suggests, an enormous Christmas pudding! Indeed, it is still possible to see proofs of his work in the Norwich Castle museum on which he had pencilled such remarks as 'Not my lettering' and 'Not my colours.' At an early stage his work came to the attention of Mr John Shaw Hopkins, a director of Caley's who greatly encouraged him, and Hopkins became a regular patron and took him on many trips to the Continent. On his first visit abroad at the age of eighteen Munnings was taken to the 1900 Leipzig Fair (via The Hague, Amsterdam and Berlin) where A.J. Caley had a trade stand and where Munnings was required to paint and design posters on the spot, some of which could well have been to advertise and promote the company's products, including possibly crackers. While not actually featured in this book, there is an early Munnings painting of the ornate Caley stand at that same Leipzig fair. Whether it was during that trip or not I have been unable to establish, but he also visited Dresden, Frankfurt, Dusseldorf and Munich, presumably also with Mr Hopkins.

Caley's itself had originally been formed by Alfred Jarman Caley – a chemist who came to Norwich in 1857 and operated from premises in London Street. By 1863, he was producing his mineral waters as a profitable sideline. His business expanded greatly with the addition of chocolate and ice cream to his product range, necessitating a move to Bedford Street close by. The year 1890 saw the company starting to operate from an ever-expanding factory at Chapel Field, which became known as the Fleur De Lys works.

FROM LEFT TO RIGHT *Albert Jarman Caley – founder of Caley's of Norwich; Edward J. Caley, director – son of A.J. Caley; Frederick W. Caley, director – nephew of A.J. Caley.*

Due to the seasonal nature of these products, and somewhere around 1898, some three years after A.J. Caley's death (Caley himself having retired from the business in 1894), his son Edward and nephew Frederick, both directors of the company, added Christmas crackers to the company's product range; a product which became a more than useful part of the business. Caley's, although not on a par with Smith's, were no mean operators in the industry and regularly supplied crackers to such far-flung markets as France, Africa, Egypt, Australia, Canada, India, China, Japan and even, if surprisingly, to Iceland!

In 1904, the Caley company was employing some 700 people to produce all its various products (including crackers). The company carried on in the family's hands until 1918 when it was taken over by the African & Eastern Trading Corporation. Despite the change of ownership, the company continued to trade under the Caley name. Until the of the merger with Tom Smith's in 1953, when the cracker-making arm of the business ceased to operate under the name of Caley's. However under the new umbrella name of Tom Smith (with CLARNICO and Mackintosh each holding fifty per cent of the shares), crackers bearing the Caley branding were still produced for a number of years.

Tom Smith's, prior to the merger with Caley's (themselves now owned by Mackintosh), were wholly owned by Clarke, Nickolls & Coombs, better known as 'CLARNICO' of confectionery fame, who had acquired the company in around 1921 at which point it seems that

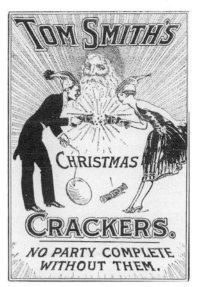

RIGHT *A typical art-deco-style advert from the 1930s advising the suitability of Tom Smith's crackers for parties and not forgetting the 'flappers'.*

BELOW *A very fancy Tom Smith's share certificate for just three shares – dated 13 April 1921. This version was in red, but a blue version, also referring to Clarke, Nickolls & Coombs (CLARNICO) is also featured in the colour section.*

the Smith family severed any of its remaining links with the company Tom had founded seventy-four years before. Today, any connection with the original Smith family is purely in the use of the brand name by its present owners.

The story of the merger between Caley's and Tom Smith's is basically as follows. As we have touched on before, the Second World War meant that both companies had to cease cracker production for the duration but a few years after hostilities had ended, Mr Eric Mackintosh of Mackintosh's (by now owners of Caley's) and Mr G.W. Morrison, chairman of Smith's, agreed in principal to merge. It was also agreed that the new joint company would operate under the name of Tom Smith's and likewise be based in Norwich. The site chosen for the new factory was at Salhouse Road and was purchased in around 1951 from the world-renowned firm Colman's (of mustard fame), during whose ownership it had been a mustard warehouse and, prior to that, an aircraft hangar in the First World War.

Caley's crackers were the first to move to the new Salhouse Road premises, followed fairly soon afterwards by Smith's, as soon as the closure of Wilson Street in London had been completed. By 1953, all formalities had been finalised and the 'new' company started its life under the chairmanship of Eric Mackintosh.

As a confectionery trading name, Caley's had pretty much ceased in overall terms when the company had been taken over by another confectionery maker, Mackintosh's of Halifax in 1932, although Caley crackers continued. However, following other takeovers by first, Rowntree, and then by Nestlé (who finally completely closed the Norwich factory in the late 1990s with the loss of some 900 jobs in a city that could ill afford it) the Caley name was resurrected by several ex-Nestlé staff who, albeit on a smaller scale, produce fine chocolate in Norwich, but sadly not the original and respected Caley crackers.

In the years leading up to the Second World War, Caley's, as far as cracker making was concerned, had not really done themselves any favours with their brochures, which were very poor efforts indeed, and the contents, although featuring much excellent design work of the period, were portrayed to a standard that did their cause no good whatsoever. They did, however, redeem themselves very slightly in 1930 with a brochure that featured a harlequin and ballerina cover design and that offered fine products such as Quaint Dutch, Owl, Ice Carnival and Boy Blue crackers. Similarly in 1939 there was a choice of cover, which featured a jester's stick with a small jester head on the end, interwoven into the Caley house logo, and which is a really superb piece of graphic design. The contents of this particular issue was, perhaps not unsurprisingly by this time, fairly similar to some of Smith's better efforts (Caley's were obviously learning!) and some of the product

ABOVE *The cracker-making department at Caley's Chapel Field factory in Norwich – pictured in 1935.*

BELOW *Again in 1935, same location, with ladies making Christmas table decorations and novelty items.*

graphics that particularly stand out are Revelry, Zuyder Zee, Jolly Tar, together with Starlight and Jewels.

The problem of poor-quality sales catalogues was one that seemed to afflict most of Tom Smith's competitors, with just about all of them being rather poor affairs with little finesse. Thus, in my opinion, the best and longest-standing cracker company had the best publicity material by far: in the particular area of sales brochures, Smith's knocked them all into a cocked hat!

Further mergers and takeovers took place over the following years involving such companies as Mead & Field (1961), Neilsons (originally an ice-cream maker) with their Festive and 'Dicky Bird' Crackers, and Mason & Church (1967) all being added to the Tom Smith's empire and indicative of the acquisitive nature of the company. Mead and Field had started operations way back in 1870 and had production units in Bishop's Stortford and Southwark. The boot was very much on

A busy scene dated 28 December 1984 taken at Smith's Salhouse Road factory as production continues apace for the coming 1985 season. In the mid to late 1980s, the company was producing around 50 million crackers each year – by far the biggest manufacturer in the world. By kind permission of Archant (Eastern Daily Press).

the other foot, however, in 1985, when the Tom Smith company was acquired for a sum of £1.3 million by Hovells of Maidstone, a long-time competitor, whose founder, it was claimed, had started cracker production in 1854 in a backyard in the Holborn area of London. At the eleventh hour it was decided that Hovells would not only to move their entire operation from Kent to the Tom Smith factory in Norwich, but would also trade under the Tom Smith brand name – an acknowledgement at that time of the kudos and respect that the company had built up in nearly 140 years of trading. The fact that the company also held several Royal Warrants was a further feather in its cap.

Another four years on and the company was subject to a manage-ment buyout, from which point the storm clouds inexorably started to gather.

At that time and towards the latter part of the 1980s while I was with the company, Tom Smith's employed in the region of 500 staff (includ-ing outworkers) split between Norwich and its subsidiary in Stockport, which had been set up in the 1950s. Between them, they were respon-sible for the annual production of some 50 million individual crackers. I'll repeat that huge figure – 50 million crackers per year! – roughly one per person across the entire nation! While many of the more expensive crackers and table decorations were still made by hand, the company also possessed two automatic cracker-making machines (automatic tying machines – ATMs), commonly accepted to be the only ones of their type at the time that could each produce nearly forty crackers per minute. This was not the first automatic method that the company had used. The patent rights for the Danish 'Willumsen' cracker-tying machine had been purchased by the company in the 1930s, with this arrangement being extended due to lack of use during the war! This machine was, in reality, a piece of equipment which aided hand tying.

Unfortunately, the company struggled for some years in the 1990s and in 1996 was taken over by Guinness Mahon & Co. A couple more years, which saw the loss of the Danson order in Canada and the even more telling loss of the large annual Sainsbury's order, proved almost certainly to be one of the final nails in the corporate coffin. Shortly thereafter, the company went into liquidation, with what was left, including the Tom Smith brand name, becoming part of the Napier Industries group of Rickmansworth, England. In yet another twist of its commercial fate with the Tom Smith's brand name, seemingly having undergone something of a metamorphosis in its fortunes for the better as part of Napier, it changed hands yet again in December 2002, with funding by Graphite Capital, a private equity firm enabling a £25m management buyout (*Sunday Times* – December 2002).

Happily, the Tom Smith name continues to flourish under its new owners although, for certain, the company is still greatly missed by many folk in the city of Norwich with whom it had a happy association for nearly fifty years. Could Tom Smith's have remained in Norwich? Well nothing is for certain in this life but it is my own opinion that had the stewardship of the firm been in more able hands, it would still be operating in the 'Fine City' to this day but that, as they say, is business!

CHAPTER ELEVEN

THE GREAT FIRE

For anybody who has ever visited or worked in a cracker factory, you will have seen just what inflammable sorts of places they are and Tom Smith's premises in Norwich were no exception.

Such is the nature of the industry that from 1 January each year, after the Christmas festivities, crackers are produced and stored for many months before being sent out for the next season's events in the late autumn. Not a very cost-effective way of business you might think, but something of a problem for many companies producing seasonal products.

Some might say that Christmas cracker factories, with so much paper, board, snaps and finished product in store, are disasters waiting to happen, and such was the case with Tom Smith's in October 1963 when a massive fire just about razed the whole of the factory to the ground.

Living in close proximity to the factory at the time, I was able to lean out of the window and watch an enormous 'firework display'. Several ladies were seen running down the road in their nightdresses to get a better view! Mr James Grimble (whose uncle William (Bill) was managing director of the company at that time) recalls:

The Great Fire. In a 1963 scene reminiscent of Guy Fawkes night, many onlookers (Tom Smith's staff among them), viewing the carnage, must have feared for their livelihoods.

My father got to hear of the fire and we jumped in the car and rushed to the factory which, when we arrived, was an inferno. Fractured gas pipes were spewing forth even more flames and all this was accompanied by a multitude of pops, bangs and explosions. Uncle William was devastated.

Happily for Uncle William and indeed the rest of the employees the new, rebuilt factory was up and running again in just about a year!

CHAPTER TWELVE

THE CHANGING MARKETPLACE

OLD FAVOURITES & NEW IDEAS

During my time with Tom Smith's in the late 1980s, I was responsible for the conception and develpoment of a number of new ideas such as Dinner Party and Pot Pourri crackers and the re-introduction of several Victorian-style box designs, all of which were quite well received by the great cracker-buying public. However, such is the march of progress that the younger generation at that time were, and probably still are, more interested in such things as Postman Pat, Thomas the Tank Engine and Paddington Bear to name but a few of what are known as 'charac ter' crackers. Old favourites such as Jim Henson's Muppets, Jungle Book and Thunderbirds crackers had their day, although conversely, there has now developed a revival and great collecting demand for anything to do with Thunderbirds!

These, in turn, were superseded by such designs as garden and wild flower crackers (both of which as a novelty contained packets of seeds), together with indoor firework crackers, 'Uncle Birthday' and jewellery crackers. Moving further on, one could find Wallace & Gromit, Russell Grant's astrological crackers and not forgetting Animates crackers which, from 1973, had featured crackers containing little porcelain miniatures of animals called 'Whimsies'. They were manufactured and supplied by the Wade factory and have become a widespread collecting hobby in their own right. Sadly, certainly for collectors, these popular crackers were initially discontinued when Tom Smith's were taken over by Napier in 1998 but, in response to this commercial setback, Wades themselves filled the gap and today offer their own crackers, which they have specially packed with their sought-after 'Whimsies'. The collectors are smiling again! Coming right up to date, crackers have not escaped the ubiquitous clutches of one Harry Potter and friends, whose brand image adorns at least one box currently on offer.

'CRACKERS? CERTAINLY MADAM.'

For more than a century and a half, there have been countless retail stockists of crackers but for the purposes of this book, I would like to concentrate on just two of the bigger names, namely Selfridges who, from its very beginning in 1909, stocked a great many varieties of crackers including a number produced by Tom Smith's, and Gamages, that other well-known London store.

In these days of 'own branding', manufacturers' names are usually not publicised but early Selfridges catalogues indicate that Tom Smith's name certainly must have been mentioned as it was invariably an integral part of the Smith's box graphics, with certain designs indisputably appearing in both companies' catalogues.

As detailed elsewhere in this story, Tom Smith's themselves often offered designs of a somewhat dubious racial nature and in this area, Selfridges were also no exception. At the beginning they would offer such Christmas novelties as 'The Harmless Lunatic – A nigger seated upon a barrow – energetically propels it backwards – Clever and Amusing.' Similarly, a mechanical Christmas novelty figure on offer was referred to as 'The Crazy Nig'. All unacceptable descriptions in today's terms but, as previously noted, it was a different era then, with different attitudes and values.

In those early years Selfridges amazingly offered the public a selection of around seventy basic crackers, usually in boxes of twelve with prices ranging from just 5½d up to 6s 6d. Added to this was a whole further series of Novelty, Floral, French Jewel, Firework, Topical, Monster, Tug of War and Midget crackers, all of which swelled the range by more than another thirty varieties. And while Tom Smith's

TOM SMITH'S SIGNALLING CRACKERS.
No. 3115.

An amusing Game. A Cardboard Model of a Boy Scout with Signalling Flags, Pistol and Shots are placed into a box containing 9 Crackers, together with instructions how to play. The Crackers contain Hats, Caps, Toys, Signalling Instruction Books, Scout Cinematograph, etc.

Per dozen boxes **12/-**

Another Scouting theme with what seems to be quite a dangerous little toy pistol and shots included in this box of 'Signalling Crackers'. On the face of it, the scout appears to have been set up as the target in this 1910–11 presentation.

may not have been supplying them all, they must have been doing very good business with the store at that time.

The Tug of War crackers, in particular, were rather unusual in that they were pulled by 'long ropes or cords – causing much amusement' and something never seen these days. Selfridges' Symphony Orchestra crackers with headdresses and musical toys were also a nice touch and for the Scouting fraternity, one could purchase Boy Scout crackers – 'representing Our Little Friends of all the World'.

I think it is also worth mentioning some of the other weird and wonderful names on offer from the store at that time such as: Always Merry and Bright, Stilton Cheese, Fairy Lamps, Little Hollander and Winter Logs. The 'Grown-Up' cracker range (adults only) included: Dickens, Box of Cigars, Naval and Military, *Entre Nous* and Found in a Taxi. What the cracker makers of the day decided would or could be found in a taxi, heaven only knows! And of the topical range there were available Happy Old Age Pensioners (with limited sales appeal these days I would suggest!), Signs of the Times, Votes for Women and Indian Empire, while the Mammoth (Monster) crackers were to be had in sizes up to five or six feet long and containing over 100 novelties each. Another early catalogue list shows novelty crackers with such names as:

House Tops, South Pole, Carnival, Louis Wain (after the eccentric cat painter), Iced Cakes and Aeroplanes, and yet another offers Cricketers, Aviators, Motor Goggles, Bridge, Thought Reading, Toy Orchestra and Pantomime Rehearsal – the list is seemingly endless!

Concerning the crackers that they had on offer, Selfridges would advise customers:

> *Dainty, ingenious and artistic, these seasonable specialities become more and more indispensable. One hardly knows which to admire most – the excellent, varied contents, or the beautifully brilliant designs that enclose them. Huge assortments are now on view in the Confectionery Department, and an early selection is urged, as many varieties cannot be repeated.*

Fred Redding – who for many years looked after the Selfridges archive – tells that it was the strategy of the founder, Mr Harry Selfridge, to appeal greatly to the upper classes in those opening years. He was much in contact with the smart set, nobility and even Royalty and was always keen to employ people from the 'upper classes'. To imagine Lady So-and-So or the Honorable Such-and-Such selling crackers to ever-so-'umble Joe Bloggs in a large department store is an amusing concept to say the least.

And then there was Gamages. Just as with Selfridges, this large well-known store sold countless thousands of boxes of crackers over the years, with archive material showing that in 1910–1912 the company catalogue featured six fully illustrated pages. I have been unable to discover whether the store was purely a retailer of the product or whether it manufactured its own but, whichever was the case, it was certainly turning over large quantities of stock. It is also known that in 1913 the store offered crackers featuring designs by Lawson Wood, the well-known artist whose work was also featured on postcards of the same period. It is said that these designs were patented but I feel that this claim probably refers more to copyright or the trademark of the artist's work.

TODAY'S MARKETPLACE

Here, at the beginning of the twenty-first century, while many crackers are themed – linking them invariably, under licence to current film or game trends for the young, one can still find the more traditional type of cracker or table decoration using the same types of materials with which Tom Smith would have been so familiar. Currently, south coast manufacturer 'House of Crackers' are keeping the tradition alive with their beautiful period reproductions of the original Victorian and Edwardian style crackers which Smiths were producing some hundred years ago.

While in the main, with crackers still fulfilling their traditional Christmas role, almost all the current generation of cracker manufacturers channel at least some of their energies into producing crackers that target such areas as anniversaries, parties for children, weddings, dinner parties and indeed any type of function as well as the themed type of cracker already mentioned.

The Christmas cracker is now known in very many parts of the world. Japan in particular shows significant interest in anything to do with traditional English and other European Christmas material and ephemera.

Today, crackers are also exported to numerous countries across the world – each with its own individual marketing requirements. In the USA, for instance, as previously mentioned, many of our American cousins tend to think of crackers as a biscuit you eat with cheese and certainly during my time in the cracker industry also tended to be very cautious, indeed some might say hostile from an import point of view, about the 'explosive' content of the snaps! For export to some countries, manufacturers have to take into account the fact that by tradition, certain colours may be unlucky, have perhaps religious connections or associations and represent something totally different from what they may suggest in Great Britain. Such are the vagaries of plying your wares on the international marketplace!

Today, at least some crackers for the North American market are today produced in Canada. In France they are known as *pétards de Noël*, and who would have thought they would have found a market in the sands of the Middle Eastern Gulf states? Indeed, many ex-patriot English people who have settled the four corners of the globe have taken the cracker tradition with them as instanced by their use in South Africa. While in general, markets ebb and flow, the hugely populated and largely untapped Chinese market must offer very significant opportunities to spread Tom Smith's invention even further afield in the future, although during the writing of this book, I have noticed many crackers that have been manufactured in China (with its lower manufacturing costs) making the journey in reverse and being offered for sale in at least one large UK supermarket chain! However, it could be that the Christmas cracker is far too much of a peculiarly English tradition to remotely stand much chance of catching on in places such as China!

CHAPTER THIRTEEN

PERSONAL RECOLLECTIONS

I t is always of interest to hear the personal recollections of people who actually worked within a given industry. One of those in question is Val Bartley, a master of the art of cracker making, who was in charge of Tom Smith's sample room in Norwich between 1965 and 1997 and who, in her many years with the company, produced literally hundreds of thousands of superb hand-made cracker samples for existing or potential customers, and for all sectors of society from the highest to the most humble.

Val, who herself started on the factory floor before moving to manage the Sample Room, recalls:

> *The first step as part of our service to our customers was to supply samples – either to the customer's own choice of colours and materials, or by offering our own suggestions. My team and I were continuously called upon to produce samples and customers would include such well-known retail organisations as Sainsbury's, Boots and John Lewis. We once had to produce prototypes of a novelty van for Harrods which subsequently went into full production.*

Val and her colleagues were often called upon to demonstrate the art of cracker making at various retail outlets during the run-up to the Christmas period.

The company, having the Royal Warrants, would always produce the annual Christmas cracker requirements for the Royal family. Contents for the crackers were always kept a well-guarded secret but now Val reveals:

In reality, the Royal cracker contents were not really very much different from the normal crackers at the top end of our range. We never included jewellery or pewter by Royal request but would frequently use such items as pill boxes, onyx eggs, key rings and silk scarves etc.

Three cases of samples containing eight varieties of table decorations and twelve varieties of 'pulling' crackers, as they were known, were sent to the Royal household for a selection to be made. That being done, we did the rest!

On another occasion, we had to produce individual 'his 'n' hers' table decoration crackers for the Charles and Diana wedding. The crackers were basically white and silver and were presented within beautiful silk-lined presentation boxes (supplied by a local jeweller) with a see-through perspex cover. The contents were a silver brooch for her and cufflinks for him. Whether the Royal couple ever actually pulled them I never did hear, but it was a thrill to be involved with them.

Val recalls yet another occasion when crackers had to be made for President and Mrs Ronald Reagan to celebrate their last Christmas at the White House:

The company sent a box of six crackers, produced to replicate the American flag – the Star Spangled Banner – all in red, white and blue and it was fun to think that my work may have finished up in the Oval Office!

As a result of all her efforts over many years of producing wonderful crackers, and with the company being a member of the Royal Warrant Holders Association (and to celebrate that organisation's 150th anniversary), Val and her husband were invited, as part of a delegation from Tom Smith's, to one of the celebrated garden parties at Buckingham Palace in July 1990. 'It was a very posh clothes affair and advance notice was given that we had to wear hats and gloves!' recalls Val.

The party was graced by the Queen, Prince Phillip, the Queen Mother and several of the lesser Royals – Prince Charles being unable

ABOVE *Val Bartley –
Sample Room supervisor
and a Tom Smith stalwart
for many years at their
Norwich factory.*

RIGHT *The late Matilda
Kitson – a doyenne of
the cracker industry, who
served Tom Smith's for
fifty years. What Matilda
didn't know about
Christmas crackers wasn't
worth knowing.*

to attend. But the highlight, however, was the presence of the lovely Princess Diana. 'She looked absolutely stunning in a red suit with cream lapels and had the most gorgeous complexion,' Val remembers. 'Photographs were not permitted but I shall never forget that most special of days. I wonder if Tom Smith ever got to meet the Royals of his day?'

We move on now to Mrs Matilda Kitson, who was a stalwart of the Tom Smith company for fifty years. Matilda, born in the Mile End area of London, remembered how she started work in 1921 with the company being run at that time by Dolly and Tom Smith (the younger). Skinning almonds for marzipan followed by fondant dipping did nothing to advance her artistic ambitions but after some six months, she was able to transfer to the cracker section. It didn't pay a fortune.

*Pay in fact was very low and I was only able to earn between 4½d and 6d
[1½p to 2½p in today's terms] per gross. Having become more experienced,*

I was able to make or 'tie' as it was known, six gross or 864 crackers per day. The variety was enormous with many different designs and styles and the work was very hard. I also remember the paper hats of those days which were very different from those of today. They were much more based on 'proper' hats and were made on real hat makers' stands. The materials were all much better than those used now.

Matilda recalled that 'special' crackers once included some for the then Prince of Wales which had his feather emblem attached. On another occasion, she had to prepare crackers for the passengers onboard the *Union Castle* liner. Matilda eventually moved down to Norwich when the company merged with Caley's in 1953. In an amazing career of five decades with the company, she worked, at various times, on all the many stages of cracker production and was rightly known as the ultimate authority and fount of all knowledge on all things relating to Tom Smith and his crackers.

Just as my search for local, pre-1953 Caley's employees seemed to be falling on stony ground, St Snappy – patron saint of cracker makers (only joking, folks) – came to my rescue. In Lily Brown, I discovered a source of information concerning the earlier years of Caley crackers in Norwich. Lily, an amazingly sprightly and joyous lady in her ninetieth year when I interviewed her, was a mine of information and possibly the oldest surviving employee of the pre-1953 merger with Tom Smith's.

Lily recalls:

Times were pretty difficult when I was a youngster and work was quite hard to find. I joined Caley's straight from school at the age of fourteen in 1926. They always took on quite a lot of school leavers and the cracker section was in the part of the chocolate factory which overlooked Chapel Field gardens. We liked being there because we could chat up the boys out of the window!

We didn't have any union representation in those days but the working conditions were not too bad, although if you were even just one minute late for work you were kept outside the gate for a further fifteen minutes and the money for that time was deducted from your wages. The wages were poor in those days and I got 8s 4d [about 42p in today's money] per week, although when you got more experienced in making crackers you could go on to piece work and get your money up to around 15s [75p]. It was pretty boring and repetitive work and our working day was from 8 a.m. until 6 p.m. but could be longer if there were rush orders to get out. There was usually a slack period each year around June and July and we were often laid off for a time. The company didn't pay us any money during this period and we had to fill in with something else until the orders picked up and we were taken back on.

While a few men were employed, although not directly in making the crackers, I seem to remember that there were around 100 girls in our section and there were four of us to a bench. The total workforce in the Caley factory at this time was in the region of 1,000. We were treated reasonably well but the charge hands were pretty strict. Our crackers were always inspected and if considered below par had to be done again, which was not so good if you were on piece work.

Before Tom Smith's came on the scene I remember that many of the crackers we produced were pretty plain affairs, but after we merged with them they became much brighter and more interesting with some lovely designs.

We did get the weekends off but there was not really much by way of social welfare in the factory and there was no such thing as safety clothing like there is today. We just wore plain overalls over our normal clothes. Did we get any perks? Well, we could always buy a bag of Caley's chocolate 'seconds' and at Christmas they gave us a box of crackers – talk about coals to Newcastle!

Most of us were young and there was always a happy atmosphere. When I had my family I still used to make crackers at home as an outworker and produced mini tree crackers, but eventually went to work at the new factory at Salhouse Road.

I don't remember many accidents at work as it was not really the most dangerous type of occupation, but there was one occasion when one of the girls caught her hand in the automatic cracker-making machine and was quite badly hurt. I didn't hear of her getting any compensation.

I finally retired in 1972 and have no idea as to just how many crackers I actually made in my time, but it must have been hundreds of thousands. Best of all I shall always remember being surrounded by all my girl friends and colleagues and singing away to 'Music while you work' on the wireless among the great piles of coloured crêpe paper, snaps and novelties. It was like Christmas day every day.

It had been a pleasure to talk to Lily and, just to cap my visit, she produced a wonderful framed Caley's 'See-Saw' crackers box lid, still in its original vibrant colours. It features two children sitting at each end of a giant cracker which they are using as a see-saw, and at the fulcrum balances a white duck – a typical piece of graphic design of its period and, like Lily, one of the few survivors.

Mrs Alice Howman of Norwich remembers starting at Caley's in 1935 at the age of fourteen straight from school.

My job was to fill Christmas net stockings with little toys. My hands got red raw due to the roughness of the netting and I didn't like it very much as it was so repetitive.

For her sore hands and the boredom, Alice received the princely sum of 7s 6d (37½p) per week (and some ointment!).

CHAPTER FOURTEEN

THE PAST & THE FUTURE

T he following dates are approximate and give the reader a rough guide to the various innovations and improvements made by Tom Smith and subsequently his family within the cracker industry that he had founded.

1847   The Sugared Almond developed from the original French bonbon format to include a love motto and twisted ends.

1850   The Almond disappears and is replaced by various toys, trinkets and jewellery.

1860   The basic shape of the cracker evolves to pretty much as we know it today and the 'snap' or detonator is introduced.

1880   Colour co-ordinated crackers and boxes are introduced.

1890   The introduction of crackers made out of crêpe paper takes place.

1900   Crackers with floral decorations are introduced.

1910   Colourful centrepieces with crackers as decorations are introduced.

1912   Printed designs on crêpe paper wrappers are introduced.

1933   Printed individual designs on foil wrappers are introduced.

1934   The 'ultimate' double-snap cracker is introduced (although this appears not to have caught the public imagination).

THE FUTURE

What is the future of the Christmas cracker? In asking that question, perhaps we should ask what is the future of Christmas itself as we know it. Certainly for me, the 'golden age' of crackers was between 1880 and 1930 with the quality and variety of product and of course the stunning artworks and graphics offering the public a choice that sadly does not even remotely exist today. In Victorian times and even into the earlier years of the twentieth century when computers, computer games, radios, TV, the ubiquitous mobile phone and even motor cars were just a figment of the imagination, perhaps Christmas really was the traditional celebration that we in the twenty-first century imagine it used to be. That being the case, then just maybe there was a ready-made place for the humble Christmas cracker in that era – a marketing niche just waiting to be exploited. Simple amusement and homely parlour fun had to be the 'norm' rather than all those technological innovations which make our modern Christmas so different. It is surely a sign of the times that the festive season today is based ever more upon commercial considerations rather than the more traditionally religious celebration of the past. But whatever your viewpoint, the fact remains that whether rich or poor, young or old, wherever and whenever during the festive season people are enjoying themselves and having fun, it will be a fairly sure bet that you will also find the traditional Christmas cracker. Long may it continue.

TOM SMITH: THE CONFECTIONER

Although Tom Smith's chief claim to fame was the invention of the Christmas cracker, it would be well to remember that, from the time that he first started out in business on his own, he was very much a confectioner. Reference to his earlier catalogues show him to have been a big player, so large and varied was his range. I have over the years seen Tom Smith referred to as a baker but there doesn't seem to be any reference to him actually having been purely a baker of bread and suchlike and I think therefore that 'confectioner' describes him more accurately. A quick glance through his separate confectionery catalogues for the years 1884 to 1887 show stunning gum-paste wedding cake ornaments (outstandingly presented against dark blue backgrounds) with the beautiful Cupid on Dolphin, Cupid & Garland, The Grecian and The Aesthetic being the pick of a very good bunch. The 1884 catalogue also shows Tom Smith's early involvement with Easter in the form of eggs decorated with young chicks and birds sitting on nests containing 'real' eggs, together with what were described at the time as Surprise eggs, Painted eggs and an empty variation that customers could open and fill for themselves. Again, little would Smith's have foreseen what a huge market Easter eggs would have become today.

Further trade catalogues from the 1890s also show an amazing array of confectionery goodies on offer, illustrating such things as: Fondant Creams à la Français (9d per lb); New York Mixture (8d per lb); Chicago Mixture (7d per lb); Tom Thumb Mixture (6d per lb); Anglo-American Caramels (9d per lb); gelatine pastilles packed in 4lb and 7lb boxes, which included bronchial jujubes, rosebud jellies, dewdrops and champagne jellies (all at between 5d and 7d per lb).

Burnt almonds, satinettes, acid drops, Chyloong ginger jellies and fruit paste confections were supplemented by the company's range of 'Penny Goods'. Sweets by the packet, jar, dozen, drum, barrel, gross and cwt were all available within the bewildering range, and in just a quick count I was able to total in excess of 175 different varieties (and/or their variations) on offer – a sweet lover's paradise.

By 1911 the range of confections, still huge, had been supplemented with a range of sweet-filled novelties, many in fancy tinplate and china containers and

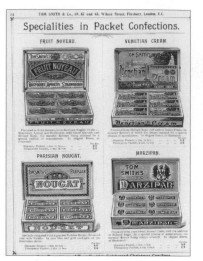

No. 4806. Gilt Basket.
200/- per doz.
See description on next page.

FROM LEFT TO RIGHT

A typical Tom Smith's 1906–07 catalogue page showing four presentations of confectionery packaging and prices from the hundreds available.

'Flowering' crackers featured in this particularly nice basket novelty display from 1928–29. Maybe a Christmas idea for some of today's enterprising flower arrangers?

A superb mechanical counter or window display novelty dated 1891–92 in the guise of a Japanese lady (or Geisha?) – just one small example of the many, now highly collectible novelties offered by Tom Smith's over the years.

which even then numbered over ninety. From trains to teapots, banjos to boots – they were all there and are highly sought after by the collectors of today.

Mr Bob Morrison, for many years the Tom Smith company chief executive, confirms that a decision was made just prior to the start of the Second World War that the company would cease to market confectionery and cake decorations, and concentrate almost entirely on crackers and associated Christmas products. That said, reference to catalogues of the early to mid-1930s indicate that sweets, novelties and general confections were still substantially available, and all those little old-fashioned sweet shops that many of us as youngsters remember on every corner in every town must have been bursting at the seams with many of the goodies produced or supplied by Tom Smith's.

HONOURS AND PATRONAGE

ROYAL WARRANTS

During the twentieth century, Tom Smith's had the honour to be granted a number of Royal Warrants, which are listed as follows:

1906   Tom Smith's was granted the Prince of Wales' Warrant.

1909   In October Tom Smith's became a member of the Royal Warrant Holders Association.

1910   In December George V granted Tom Smith's his warrant as suppliers of Christmas crackers. This was the first time that Tom Smiths held a warrant for a reigning monarch.

1911   On 23 March Tom Smith's was granted Queen Mary's Royal Warrant as manufacturers of Christmas crackers. This warrant was renewed in 1938 and was held by Tom Smith's until Queen Mary's death in 1953.

1964   Queen Elizabeth II's warrant was granted on 1 January.

1975   Queen Elizabeth the Queen Mother's Warrant was granted on 10 March.

1987   The Prince of Wales' Warrant was granted on 1 January.

2003   At the time of compiling this list, I am advised by the Royal Warrant Holders Association that the current owners of the Tom Smith brand name still hold the warrants for both Queen Elizabeth II and surprisingly also for Queen Elizabeth the Queen Mother, which, following her mother's death, the current monarch has permitted to remain in place only until 2007.

Tom Smith's became a member of the Royal Warrant Holders Association in 1909, although its membership lapsed between the death of Queen Mary in 1953 and receiving Queen Elizabeth II's Warrant in 1964. Being Norfolk-based for well over forty years it was appropriate that the company was also a member of the Sandringham Branch of the Royal Warrant Holders Association. Today, the long tradition of supplying crackers to the Royal

Household continues in the hands of Napier – the current owners of the Tom Smith name. As with all things Royal, discretion has always been the byeword and the cracker contents were kept secret – as recalled by Val Bartley in 'Personal Recollections'. However, Val reveals all in her book, so the Royal secret is secret no longer!

EXHIBITIONS AND MEDALS

Like many companies, Tom Smith's was not backward in promoting its product range and from 1876 (and probably well before that date) the company was attending various exhibitions and winning numerous gold and silver medals for the quality of its products.

The following list shows details of known medals awarded between 1876 and 1908, followed by a reproduction of a picture of the company's trade stand at the 1908 Franco-British Exhibition in London.

1876 Philadelphia International Exhibition (awarded by United States Centennial Commission) – gold and silver medals for purity.
1882 London International Food Exhibition.
1895 London Empire of India Exhibition.
1896 Empire of India and Ceylon Exhibition.
1897 Victoria Era Exhibition★ promoted by London Exhibitions Limited.
1898 London International Universal Exhibition at Earl's Court.
1908 London Franco-British Exhibition – gold medal.

★This exhibition was purely for confectionery and Smith's had six exhibits overall. There was a 'Model Factory' in the Ducal Hall and others in The Empress Theatre, The Imperial Gardens, Elysia, Western Gardens and the Great Wheel.

The highly ornate Tom Smith's stand at the 1908 London Franco-British Exhibition. There was still a great deal of space devoted to cake decorations and ornaments at this time.

MAJOR QUALITY & MISS SWEETLY

Strange things often turn up when one gets into the world of historical research and while I don't particularly want to spend time talking about confectionery, Amoret Tanner of Reading University has presented me with something of a poser.

Many readers will, I'm sure, remember the images of the soldier and the girl (Major Quality and Miss Sweetly as they were known) that confectionery manufacturers John Mackintosh and subsequently Rowntree Mackintosh used for many years as the imagery for their world-famous Quality Street brand. Having been involved with this company's design work for some twenty-three years, I have personally worked on and with these characters on countless packaging and promotional projects. I know them well. You can imagine therefore my surprise upon receiving a copy of Amoret's superb Tom Smith's catalogue cover for 1934–35, to find both figures prominently displayed in the centre of the design, representing not Quality Street but Christmas crackers! I was very taken aback by this and of course it raised questions in my mind.

Quality Street itself, so I am told, was originally introduced in around 1936 and so in view of the date of the Smith's catalogue, one wonders which of the two companies first came up with the idea for the soldier and the girl. Commercially it's hard to believe that one company would allow the other to use its own product branding and so maybe it was simply the age-old case of plagiarism – who knows? On the other hand, there has been quite a lot of antique ephemera over the years featuring soldiers and girls, and so this 'coincidence' may indeed be just that.

Another tenuous possibility is that, conceivably, both companies just happened to source the material from the same artist or designer although on close inspection, it strikes me that the image could well be a montage of several separate design elements. Whatever the origins, there, smiling out and holding examples of the older style crackers with fringed ends, are these two Quality Street-style figures as may be seen in the colour section of this book. Maybe I am just imagining things and am mistaken. Maybe it is just one of life's little coincidences but the similarity is such that I think not. Thanks however to Amoret for the 'find' and I shall go on puzzling!

Appendix Four

THE CASTLE OF THE CRACKER KING

In seeking out information for this book, many stones have been turned and one in particular unearthed a delightfully flowery article with the fairytale-like title of 'The Castle of the Cracker King'. It was written in 1911 by E.M. Tait following a visit to Tom Smith's Wilson Street factory and published in *The Lady* magazine in November of that year. Flowery the article may be, but notwithstanding, it gives an interesting and certainly humorous angle on the cracker industry of over ninety years ago and is reproduced here exactly as it was originally written.

The tree groaned and quivered as the great two-handled saw cut steadily through its trunk.

'Why am I being tortured like this? What will become of me?'

The wood nymph heard and answered –

'This is but the beginning of great adventures and many changes, and at the last you will give joy to someone. Have patience. Wait and see. All will be as I say.'

She was very wise, but she could not tell all she knew. Wise folk never can.

  Far away on the other side of the world the rice stalks whispered and shivered as they fell before the sickle.

'What is happening? What will become of us?'

The earth-mother heard and answered –

'Hush! This is but the beginning of great adventures and many changes. The grain will give food, the straw will give pleasure to my human children. Therefore ye are blessed. Have patience. Wait and see. All will be as I say.'

She was very wise, with the wisdom of all the ages, but she also could not tell all she knew. Wise folk never can.

  While the tree was felled and the rice was reaped other strange things were happening in many parts of the world, where men were busy in pits and quarries and mines, digging and hewing and blasting, getting stone and clay and sand, saltpetre and soda and sulphur, gold and silver, tin and copper. Always the clay and the stone and the sand, the metals and minerals complained when they were torn from their beds, and the gnomes heard and answered —

'Hello! What's all this grumbling about? This is only the beginning of all you've got to go through, and you won't know yourselves at last, for you'll be quite gay and handsome. It doesn't seem possible, but it's true.'

The gnomes are as wise as the wood nymphs and the earth mother, but they are not at all sympathetic. Gnomes never are.

The adventures and changes went on unceasingly, and so many and so wonderful they were that, if the whole story was written, no book in the world would be big enough to hold it. Also the tree, and hundreds and thousands of its brother and sister trees as well, and the rice straw, the stones and clay and sand, the metals and minerals, and lots of all sorts of other things, wax and oil, and cotton and wool and silk, and even the hides and hoofs of beasts — everything you can think of, and a great many more besides — were constantly meeting and mingling with each other, and every time they did that, something happened to them that made them different from what they had been before.

So it went on, until they were all gathered together in one place, a great building in the heart of London City, which is the Castle of the Cracker King, though ordinary people call it just Tom Smith's factory. For the trees and the straw, the stones and clay and sand, the metals and minerals, and all the others — everything you can think of and a great many more besides — were all wanted to make Christmas crackers.

From the uttermost parts of the earth they had come. They had passed through fire and water, through heat and cold, and on the way they had provided work — and that also means heat and happiness — for hundreds of thousands of men and women and children. And now here they were, but so changed that they did not know themselves — just as the gnomes had said they would be.

Instead of the trees and straw, there were piles of paper, crepe paper and glazed paper, fragile, transparent gelatine paper (which is always rather inclined to give itself airs because it is made from the hoofs and hides of animals, and not from wood and straw pulp like the others) in all colours of the rainbow, gorgeous red and orange and yellow, delicate blue and pink, green and mauve. There were strips of fancy paper blazoned with gold and silver, pure white paper for linings, thousands of brilliant birds and butterflies and quaint, gaily costumed little figures for decorating the outsides of the crackers, animal masks and funny faces for putting inside them, all stamped and printed on thicker paper, more thousands of hats and caps, helmets and costumes, and of tiny umbrellas and lanterns, fans and paper toys, stacks of cardboard boxes, and of beautiful coloured pictures for the lids.

Then, instead of the stones and the clay and the sand, of the metals and minerals and all the other things, there were multitude of tiny vases of china and Bohemian glass, *jewellery of all kinds, rings and brooches, chains and bracelets and toy watches, and dear little 'lucky charms', cunningly made from glass and metal, little motor cars and trams, fire engines and aeroplanes, guns and warships; fireworks , too, and puzzles and games – everything you can think of, and a great many more besides. And some of them were made in Holland and Germany, Sweden and Switzerland, Russia and Bohemia – that's where the coloured glass that looks so like real jewels comes from – others in America, and others, again, in Egypt and India and Burma and far Japan, and a great many here in England; in Birmingham and Coventry and London City itself.*

Every working day all the year round a mighty whirr and hum is heard throughout the Castle of the Cracker King. That is from the great machines which are printing and stamping, cutting, and fringing the paper, for everything of that kind is done in the castle itself. At one machine, which has a curious knife like a long, narrow steel ribbon, a man does nothing else but cut out shapes for paper hats and caps, helmets and costumes, hundreds at a time, which are fashioned and pasted, trimmed, and folded by girls, who work so quickly and neatly that the pretty things seem to grow like magic under their clever fingers.

But the most fascinating places in the castle are the big white-walled rooms where the crackers are actually made and finished. Here at long counters sit scores of pretty girls, each with all the materials for the particular kind of cracker she is making ranged in front of her. You wouldn't think there were over seventy separate parts to be put together for every ordinary box of crackers, and more in the very elaborate ones, would you? As the gnomes said, 'It doesn't seem possible, but it's true.'

There are twelve outside papers, twelve white petticoats or linings, twenty-four fancy end–papers, twelve strips of cardboard, each with its wad of gunpowder in the centre – the detonator that makes the 'bang' – twelve fancy surprise articles, and the scrap picture that gives the finishing touch.

The girls lay the different papers one over the other in their proper order, fixes the fancy ends with a smear of glue, rolls the set of papers round a brass tube, slips in the detonator, ties the other end; slips in the 'surprise,' ties the other end, sticks on the scrap, and there is the cracker. It is all done so swiftly – in less time than it takes to tell – that the heap of finished crackers grows as if by magic, just like the paper caps do in other rooms.

The girls are busy and blithe as bees. Indeed, there is a general air of jollity about everyone in the Cracker King's castle, which is just as it ought to be.

And so, packed snug and safe in their boxes, the crackers set out on the last and greatest and happiest adventure of all. For, as the things of which they are made came from every part of the world, so they, twenty-five million of them this very Christmas – are sent all over the world again on their wonderful mission, which is to make fun and frolic and merriment in millions of homes, from the humblest to the greatest.

Perhaps the crackers which you and I shall pull so gaily when Christmas comes round are being made in the Castle at this very moment; so they arrive in time for

Christmas wherever they are going, and that is to every place under the sun where the British flag flies or the British language is spoken.

By many strange ways they go before they reach journey's end. For they are carried across the desert sands of Egypt on camelback, through the Indian and Burmese jungles on elephants, over African veldt in creaking wagons, drawn by the long, slow ox teams. They go to the lone homesteads on the Canadian prairies, to the fur trappers in the frozen North, to solitary stations and huts in the Australian back blocks and the New Zealand bush, and to many a lovely, remote island in the South Seas, where they bring memories of England and home to the exiles who keep their Christmas under the tropic skies.

We all know the end of the story. Laughter and glee, fusillades of 'cracks,' an eager search for the hidden treasure, and the crackers have vanished.

The litter of gaily coloured paper fragments is gathered up and burnt. The tiny toys and picture scraps are treasured for a while − sometimes for minutes or hours, sometimes for years − but all, sooner or later, by one way or another, go back to the bosom of mother earth whence they came, and there become changed once more. For nothing in this wonderful world really perishes; not even the ashes of the burnt paper, though it seems to us they do.

But, whenever you look at the little cracker toys that you keep − some of them in your doll's house or play boxes, perhaps − or tiny vases and ornaments on a little shelf; or when you use the picture-scraps for actors and actresses in your toy theatre − they come in splendidly for that − or paste them up in the pretty scrapbooks that poor little boys and girls in hospitals love to have − remember their wonderful history, and all the many adventures and changes they went through before they were made from the trees and the straw, the stones and the clay and the sand, the metals and minerals − everything you can think of and a great many more besides!

If you are interested in purchasing
other books published by Tempus, or in case you have
difficulty finding any Tempus books in your local bookshop, you can
also place orders directly through our website

www.tempus-publishing.com

Similarly, if you would like to know any more about the history
of the Christmas cracker or the authors' special education pack for
schools, he can be reached at:

www.thekingofcrackers.co.uk

or email:
info@thekingofcrackers.co.uk